S0-BDM-221

ESPECIALLY FOR

....

FROM

....

DATE

....

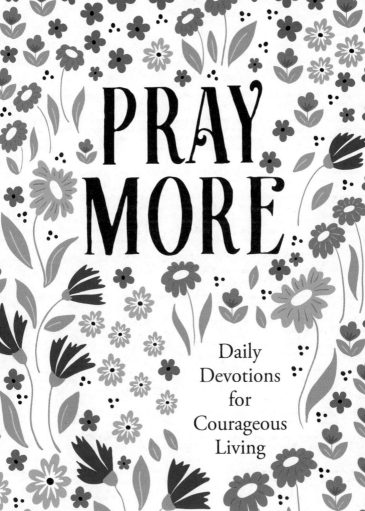

PRAY MORE

Daily
Devotions
for
Courageous
Living

BARBOUR
PUBLISHING

© 2021 by Barbour Publishing, Inc.

Print ISBN 978-1-63609-045-0

eBook Edition: Adobe Digital Edition (.epub) 978-1-63609-231-7

All rights reserved. No part of this publication may be reproduced or transmitted for commercial purposes, except for brief quotations in printed reviews, without written permission of the publisher.

Churches and other noncommercial interests may reproduce portions of this book without the express written permission of Barbour Publishing, provided that the text does not exceed 500 words or 5 percent of the entire book, whichever is less, and that the text is not material quoted from another publisher. When reproducing text from this book, include the following credit line: "From *Pray More: Daily Devotions for Courageous Living*, published by Barbour Publishing, Inc. Used by permission."

Readings compiled from *Worry Less, Pray More*; *Stress Less, Pray More*; and *Fear Less, Pray More*. Published by Barbour Publishing, Inc. All rights reserved.

Scripture quotations marked NLT are taken from the *Holy Bible*. New Living Translation copyright© 1996, 2004, 2015 by Tyndale House Foundation. Used by permission of Tyndale House Publishers, Inc. Carol Stream, Illinois 60188. All rights reserved.

Scripture quotations marked MSG are taken from *THE MESSAGE*, copyright © 1993, 2002, 2018 by Eugene H. Peterson. Used by permission of NavPress. All rights reserved. Represented by Tyndale House Publishers, Inc.

Scripture quotations marked KJV are taken from the King James Version of the Bible.

Scripture quotations marked NASB are taken from the New American Standard Bible®, Copyright © 1960, 1971, 1977, 1995, 2020 by The Lockman Foundation. All rights reserved.

Scripture quotations marked NIV are taken from the HOLY BIBLE, NEW INTERNATIONAL VERSION®. NIV®. Copyright © 1973, 1978, 1984, 2011 by Biblica, Inc.™ Used by permission. All rights reserved worldwide.

Scripture quotations marked NKJV are taken from the New King James Version®. Copyright © 1982 by Thomas Nelson, Inc. Used by permission. All rights reserved.

Scripture quotations marked AMPC are taken from the Amplified® Bible, Classic Edition © 1954, 1958, 1962, 1964, 1965, 1987 by The Lockman Foundation. Used by permission.

Scripture quotations marked ESV are from The Holy Bible, English Standard Version®. Text Edition: 2016. Copyright © 2001 by Crossway, a publishing ministry of Good News Publishers. The ESV® text has been reproduced in cooperation with and by permission of Good News Publishers. Unauthorized reproduction of this publication is prohibited. All rights reserved.

Scripture quotations marked GW are taken from God's Word, Copyright © 1995, 2003, 2013, 2014, 2019, 2020 by God's Word to the Nations Mission Society. All rights reserved.

Scripture quotations marked PHILLIPS are taken from The New Testament in Modern English by J. B. Phillips copyright © 1960, 1972 J. B. Phillips God's Word to the Nations. Administered by the Archbishops' Council of the Church of England. Used by permission.

Scripture quotations marked TLB are taken from The Living Bible © 1971 by Tyndale House Foundation. Used by permission of Tyndale House Publishers, Inc., Carol Stream, Illinois 60188. All rights reserved.

Scripture quotations marked AMP are taken from the Amplified® Bible, © 2015 by The Lockman Foundation. Used by permission.

Published by Barbour Publishing, Inc., 1810 Barbour Drive, Uhrichsville, Ohio 44683, www.barbourbooks.com

Our mission is to inspire the world with the life-changing message of the Bible.

Member of the
Evangelical Christian
Publishers Association

Printed in China.

PRAY MORE!

*"Be strong. Take courage. . .because GOD,
your God, is striding ahead of you. He's right
there with you. He won't let you down;
he won't leave you."*
DEUTERONOMY 31:6 MSG

Need more courage in your life? This delightful devotional guide features daily readings and prayers designed to help you live your best life as you learn to
place your trust in the Almighty God, who gives you
courage. As you read each devotion and prayer, *Pray
More* will reinforce the truth that with God, you can
live courageously every single day—no matter what
challenges life brings your way!

Keep reading. . .and discover the courageous life
today!

WHOM SHALL I FEAR?

The LORD is my light and my
salvation; whom shall I fear?
PSALM 27:1 NASB

Fear lives next door to faith.

David's personal testimony proves he was serious about praising the Lord, yet he still pleaded with God not to hide His face from him. David's enemies stumbled and fell when they came against him, yet he asked the Lord to not deliver him into their hands. He knew God wouldn't abandon him in the days of trouble, yet his one desire was to dwell in God's presence every moment.

Like David, our one desire in life should be to dwell in God's threefold presence all the days of our lives. In God's omnipresence, we see Him everywhere we look. He dwells in us as the Holy Spirit the moment we believe in Christ, and He will never leave us. In His manifest presence, His embracing calmness soothes our souls in our darkest moments.

Teach us, O Lord, to focus on our faith in
You instead of our worldly fears and to see
Your goodness in the land of the living.

Day 2
LEVEL GROUND

Jesus said to those Jews who had believed in Him, If you abide in My word [hold fast to My teachings and live in accordance with them], you are truly My disciples. And you will know the Truth, and the Truth will set you free.
JOHN 8:31–32 AMPC

The quaking of our worlds—inner and outer—can leave us shaken. But God provides us with solutions. He helps us to be resilient, to absorb the shocks that come our way, to hold fast under the pressure.

God's Word repeatedly tells us not to be afraid. He has blessed us with the avenue of prayer. He invites and encourages us to abide in Him, promising that when we walk in His truth, when we believe His Word with our whole heart, mind, body, and soul, we are freed from the sins that snare, the worries that stress. And in so doing, we find His love spread out before us and our feet standing on level ground (see Psalm 26:3, 12).

I find my freedom in You, Lord Jesus.

TWENTY-FOUR-HOUR SECURITY

Where can I find help? My help comes from the LORD,
the maker of heaven and earth. . . . The LORD guards
you from every evil. He guards your life. The LORD
guards you as you come and go, now and forever.
PSALM 121:1–2, 7–8 GW

Imagine having a bodyguard with you twenty-four hours a day. One who is all-powerful, all-knowing. He can see the future, the present, and the past. He never sleeps or takes catnaps. He blocks the sun from scorching your skin during the day and keeps the moon's shadows from tripping you up at night. He tightly grips your hand as you walk, shielding you from all harm.

You *have* such a bodyguard. His name is God. He's all the help and protection you need. So why worry? With the Creator of the universe guarding you, surrounding you with His magnificent presence and power, nothing can touch you—in heaven or on the earth!

I rest easy, Lord, knowing You are always
with me, keeping me from harm. Thank
You for Your vigilance and protection!

VICTIM OR VICTOR— THE COURAGE TO CHOOSE

The horse is prepared for the day of battle,
but victory belongs to the LORD.
PROVERBS 21:31 NASB

The first therapeutic step after encountering a crime is to make an important decision. Do we want to cower and remain the victim, or take action and be the victor? Whether we've suffered at the hands of a bully, a scammer, or a violent criminal, facing the offender takes great courage.

As the Philistines victimized the Israelites, David's faith in the Lord gave him courage to confront Goliath. "The LORD who delivered me from the paw of the lion and the paw of the bear, He will deliver me from the hand of this Philistine" (1 Samuel 17:37 NASB).

We all have a Goliath to face. Confronting a bully, apprehending a con artist, or testifying against an assailant. God provided the right stone to make David the victor instead of the victim. Our stone is the Rock, which is Christ the Lord.

Father, as we prepare to fight our Goliaths,
help us choose to be the victor. For we know
if we want victory, we can't fight without You.

Day 5

ENLIGHTENED EYES OF FAITH

"It wasn't you who sent me here, but God."
GENESIS 45:8 GW

The Old Testament Joseph easily could have considered himself a victim of his circumstances and the people in his life. He could have blamed his brothers for throwing him in a pit and selling him to traders. He could have blamed Potiphar and his wife for his imprisonment. He could have blamed the baker and the wine bearer for leaving him to dream in the dark dungeon. But he never did. Instead, he persevered, believing that God, the Ruler of the universe, was with him, would protect him, and would turn his trials into triumphs. And so He did.

How would your outlook change if you realized that all things, people, and situations—both wonderful and awful—are part of God's plan for your life and that He will be with you through it all? Only through the enlightened eyes of your faith will you see God's caring hand in the world's darkness.

Thank You, God, for working out Your good will in all things and sticking with me through it all.

GIVING—AND GETTING—PLEASURE

Be energetic in your life of salvation. . . .
That energy is God's energy, an energy deep
within you, God himself willing and working
at what will give him the most pleasure.
PHILIPPIANS 2:12–13 MSG

Worrying can sap all your energy, using up all your strength and making you too bleary-eyed to see God's blessings, too weak to do what God's called you to do!

Dear woman, God didn't save you so that you could spend your life half asleep. He wants you to be strong, steady, and stable. So tell God all your concerns, all your imaginary what-ifs. Dig deep within, recognizing God's presence energizing you and giving you the power to let your worries melt away. Then open your eyes, and you'll see all the great tasks and blessings God has put before you.

The more you let go of your problems and pick up God's power, the more you'll please both God and yourself.

I'm digging deep, Lord, freeing my frets and
experiencing Your awesome energy! What pleasure!

FEAR OF THE SHOULD-HAVES

"Therefore, keep up your courage, men, for I believe
God that it will turn out exactly as I have been told."
ACTS 27:25 NASB

The words, "You should have. . ." are not easy to hear. They usually invoke a humble response of, "I was wrong." Those words are not always easy to say. We are blind to the future, but hindsight has 20/20 vision.

Paul warned the centurion who was in charge of him that impending danger lay ahead of the voyage. But the centurion listened to the captain and the pilot instead. They made their decision to sail based on the condition of the harbor, instead of listening to Paul, who had God's ear.

Although Paul said, "You should have listened to me," he encouraged the men because God sent an angel to disclose that all lives on board would be spared. God's plan included Paul being shipwrecked before going to Rome.

Almighty God, when we face a dreaded "should have,"
let us remember that You are still in control.
As with Paul, You will use every situation
to bring about Your plan for us.

TAKE A BREATH

*[It is] the Spirit of God that made me [which has
stirred me up], and the breath of the Almighty
that gives me life [which inspires me].*
JOB 33:4 AMPC

What do you do when the flight, fight, or freeze button has been pushed and stress has taken over? When you can't seem to get your bearings and just need a way to calm down?

Pause. Become aware of what's going on mentally, physically, spiritually, and emotionally. Remind yourself that God is with you. Then, through several deep belly breaths, reconnect with the source of all creation. Link up with the God who breathed life into you, as He did Adam (see Genesis 2:7). Find your way back to Jesus, who breathed the Word of life into His followers (see John 20:22). Recite God's words, "Be still, and know that I am God" (Psalm 46:10). Before you know it, you will feel yourself connected with the Holy Spirit (which, in Hebrew, is *ruakh*, meaning "wind" or "air in motion").

*Lord, in this breath I come to You.
Please bring peace to my soul and spirit.*

NOTHING TOO HARD FOR GOD

*Alas, Lord God! Behold, You have made the
heavens and the earth by Your great power
and by Your outstretched arm! There is
nothing too hard or too wonderful for You.*

JEREMIAH 32:17 AMPC

Sometimes the many things going *right* in your life and your world are overshadowed by that one thing that's going wrong. You begin to question whether God has the power or know-how to change things for the better or get you out of whatever mess you're in.

That's when you need to begin focusing on the right things. Trust that along with all the wonderful things God has done, is doing, and will do, He will turn any mishaps, errors, or darkness into something right, correct, and light.

You see, there is nothing too hard for God. He can do anything, so don't panic. Simply pray, and leave everything in God's mighty hands.

*Thank You, God, for reminding me nothing is too
hard for You. I'm leaving everything up to You,
knowing You'll put things right.*

SILENCE—DREAD OR DELIGHT

A time to keep silence, and a time to speak.
Ecclesiastes 3:7 nkjv

What does it mean when all the crickets in the night become silent? Danger.

All creatures hush their activities when evil lurks, or so it seems in movies. It could mean we should prepare for the dispensing of judgment, as in the thirty minutes of silence when the Lamb breaks the seventh seal.

Let us instead find delight in silence, a welcome relief after a busy day filled with beeping machines and talkative people, followed by honking traffic.

God has assigned the moments of silence and sounds. We can overcome our dread of silence in His Word. As His children, we have no fear of the judgment to come. We can delight in the quiet assurance of His forgiveness.

Dear God, our souls wait in silence for You only,
for from You comes our salvation.

Day 11
POWERFUL PAUSES

The LORD is my light and my salvation.
Who is there to fear?
PSALM 27:1 GW

Mystery writer Arthur Somers Roche wrote, "Worry is a thin stream of fear trickling through the mind. If encouraged, it cuts a channel into which all other thoughts are drained." But God would have you look to Him, rely on Him, gain your strength, confidence, and courage from Him. The key is to pause when you feel a bit unsettled. Check in with your emotions. Accept them for what they are: merely a reflection of what you're thinking.

Then become aware of what you're thinking. If your inner dialogue is against what God would have you believe, replace it with His truth. Then choose to own and live that truth. Not just in that moment but in every moment, day after day after day. By forming the habit of replacing your inner talk with God's truth, you'll soon be on His wavelength, living the life He's planned for you.

I pause, Lord, to accept my feelings, align my
thoughts with Yours, and live in Your truth.

NEVER SHAKEN

Those who trust the LORD are like Mount Zion,
which can never be shaken. It remains firm forever.
As the mountains surround Jerusalem, so the LORD
surrounds his people now and forever.
PSALM 125:1–2 GW

Sometimes worry can lead you to literally shake in your boots, but God wants you to know that if you trust in Him, you will *never* be shaken. You can stand firm, leaning on His power, confidently hoping He has a solution, one you've never even thought of—or, even better, that He's already taking care of things for you!

When you put all your trust, hope, and confidence in the God who actually *created* the mountains, you begin to feel His awesome presence surrounding you. You begin remembering all the things He has done for you and all the others who've gone before you. Knowing this, you need no longer shake in your boots but walk sure and barefooted on the highest mountains (see Psalm 18:33).

I'm trusting in You, Lord. In doing so,
I feel Your power and presence surrounding me,
enabling me to walk strong in You.

Day 13
COURAGE TO SEEK WISDOM

"For wisdom is better than jewels; and all desirable things cannot compare with her."
PROVERBS 8:11 NASB

What is the difference between knowledge and wisdom? We find knowledge in textbooks, but wisdom only comes from the Word of the Lord.

When God offered Solomon anything he wanted, the new king asked only for an understanding heart to discern between good and evil. Because Solomon asked in humility, God blessed him with wisdom as plentiful as sand on the seashore. He also rewarded him with great wealth, honor, and a long life.

We need knowledge to get through life. Reading, writing, and arithmetic provide the milk of our learning. But the meat of wisdom brings honor. If we remain content with mere book knowledge, we lose the joy of serving Him. But when we seek wisdom as though seeking silver, search for it as for hidden treasure, then He will reward us with unexpected, incomparable blessings—better than jewels.

O Lord our God, let wisdom enter our hearts and bring pleasure to our souls that we may use these divine gifts to serve You with glory and honor.

Day 14
ONE THING

"Martha, Martha, you are anxious and troubled about many things, but one thing is necessary. Mary has chosen the good portion, which will not be taken away from her."

LUKE 10:41–42 ESV

The more we worry, the less we pray. And the more we pray, the less we worry. So why not pray? But not just by saying the same old prayer over and over. Or reading the same old devotional. Or repeating the same old psalm. Instead, get some new ideas, words, books, verses. Why not actually *imagine* yourself at Jesus' feet, forgetting about all the to-dos you need to get done?

You gift a lot of people with your time, sometimes more than you have to spare! But how much of your time are you gifting to God? Take stock and stop. Sit. Listen with both ears. Choose that good part: being at your Master's feet. Gift Him with those precious moments, and He will gift you with peace of mind, body, heart, spirit, and soul.

Lord, here I am. At Your feet. Leaning back into Your presence.

Day 15

THAT SECRET PLACE

*When you pray, go into your [most] private
room, and, closing the door, pray to your
Father, Who is in secret; and your Father, Who
sees in secret, will reward you in the open.*
MATTHEW 6:6 AMPC

Women living in today's world are busy, and chances are, you're
no exception. There are kids to get on the bus, socks to find for
the husband, emails to send, projects to finish, meals to plan,
grandkids to watch, Sunday school lessons to review, dogs to
walk, and news to catch up on. Yet to be focused enough to
do all these things well, you need to unload some of the clutter
crowding your mind.

Jesus tells you to detach from the world without and the
thoughts within. Find that secret chamber He's opened just
for you where you can have a spirit-to-Spirit talk with God,
shutting yourself away from the world and shutting yourself
in with Him.

Find that place and you'll find your reward—the focus to
do and peace to be!

*Father, help me find that secret place
where it's just You and me.*

FEAR OF IGNORANCE

*For they being ignorant of God's righteousness,
and seeking to establish their own righteousness,
have not submitted to the righteousness of God.*

ROMANS 10:3 NKJV

Those who worship the false gods of this world claim to be wise. But they show their ignorance when they call Christians "knuckle-draggers" or "flat-earthers." How can they say we are descended from the knuckle-dragging ape when we believe mankind was created in the image of God? The Bible describes the earth as a circle in Isaiah 40:22. How then can they accuse Christians of once believing the earth was flat?

They say we are anti-science, yet archeologists find proof of biblical accounts in the ancient tales of Israel and other parts of the Middle East region.

In their fear of ignorance, they point accusing fingers at us, not realizing they're actually pointing to themselves. Sadly, they will remain in their fear of ignorance until they submit to the righteousness of God through the Lord Jesus Christ.

*Father God, please open the eyes of nonbelievers to
Your righteousness. Give us the courage to teach
them that wisdom comes from knowing You.*

PRACTICING TRUTH

If we claim that we experience a shared life with him and continue to stumble around in the dark, we're obviously lying through our teeth— we're not living what we claim.

1 JOHN 1:6 MSG

Winston Churchill is credited with saying, "Men occasionally stumble over the truth, but most of them pick themselves up and hurry off as if nothing ever happened." Although at first this quote may sound silly, it has the ring of truth about it.

How many times has God pointed out a truth to you, one that would help smooth your walk in this life, yet afterward, after the initial aha moment, you walked on as usual, allowing life to woo you away as if you'd never stumbled upon the truth in the first place?

God wants us walking with Jesus. The more we walk in His truth, the more light there will be for the path before us and the less stress and trip-ups we'll encounter.

What truth is God asking you to practice?

Show me, Lord, the truth You want me to live and walk in.

WORTHY THOUGHTS

*Keep your thoughts on whatever is right or deserves
praise: things that are true, honorable, fair,
pure, acceptable, or commendable.*
PHILIPPIANS 4:8 GW

It's easy to get caught up in the bad news that surrounds us: the
reports and rumors of wars, school shootings, child and spousal
abuse, drug addiction, crime, terrorism, and political strife, to
name just a few. It's enough to make you never come out from
underneath the covers. Either that or you find yourself forever
fretting about people and situations over which you have no or
little control. Yet you can't help but be concerned.

So take those news items to God. Ask Him to be in the
situation, to help the victims, to bring justice. Then leave it all in
His hands, knowing He can handle anything—and everything.
Then look for some *good* news stories—they are out there! And
fix your focus on *those* things, which are good, honorable, and
commendable, praising God in the process.

*Once I give my concerns to You, Lord, help me
fix my thoughts on those things that
deserve my praise and focus!*

COURAGE TO CONTEND WITH BULLIES

"But I tell you not to resist an evil person.
But whoever slaps you on your right cheek,
turn the other to him also."
MATTHEW 5:39 NKJV

The scene in a Christmas film with a bully terrorizing his classmates made an interesting point. The boy's favorite victim, Ralphie, became a bully himself when he used his fists to quash his enemy. But is that the way the Lord would have us contend with our oppressors?

A bully isn't always the tough kid who beats up other children. For adults, it could be a tyrannical boss, a domineering spouse, or even a pushy, well-meaning friend.

Jesus' example of responding with an attitude of kindness or a gentle answer would unsettle them more than if we'd shouted or raised a hand at them. If we love our enemies and pray for those who persecute us, then we have contended with our bullies in a way that pleases the Lord.

Gracious God, give us courage when bullies come
against us to show Your love in such a way that
they will open their hearts to You.

Day 20

HEART TO HEART

You have said, Seek My face [inquire for and require My presence as your vital need]. My heart says to You, Your face (Your presence), Lord, will I seek, inquire for, and require [of necessity and on the authority of Your Word].
Psalm 27:8 ampc

God wants you to seek His face, for He knows that when you do, your heart, mind, and spirit will have their true focus. You will find His peace, His strength, His way. You will be more in line with His will for you because you have looked to Him before you even set your foot out the door or stuck your toe in the water.

Your spirit needs God's presence just as your body needs air, food, and water. God is aching to hear your voice. He's ready for that heart-to-heart talk that will energize you for the day. Seek. Speak. Listen. Then walk.

Here I am, Lord, coming before You, seeking Your presence, breathing in Your Spirit, drinking in Your light, feeding on Your wisdom. Show me Your way.

REASSURANCE TIMES THREE

You know when I leave and when I get back; I'm never
out of your sight. . . . I look behind me and you're there, then
up ahead and you're there, too—your reassuring presence,
coming and going. This is too much, too wonderful.
PSALM 139:2, 5–6 MSG

People come and go out of your life, but there is a three-in-one
being who remains: God, Jesus, and the Holy Spirit.

Wherever you go, God sees you. Whatever you're experiencing, Jesus is familiar with it. Whatever comfort you need,
the Spirit is there, giving it to you. When you believe these
things, when you have faith in God's presence always with
you—before and behind you—all worries fade away. God is
your reassuring Protector, Jesus your undying Friend, and the
Spirit your willing Helper.

Don't worry. Pray to these three supernatural powers who
are ready, willing, and able to help you along the way.

My worries fade, Lord, and vanish into nothing
when I acknowledge Your presence, Jesus' love,
and the Spirit's power. Be with me now.

COURAGE TO SUBMIT TO AUTHORITY

For rulers are not a cause of fear for good behavior,
but for evil. Do you want to have no fear of authority?
Do what is good and you will have praise from the same.
ROMANS 13:3 NASB

Protestors refuse to accept a newly elected president. Rioters throw rocks and bottles at police. Students disregard their teachers' directives. These are only a few examples of our failure to respect authority of any kind.

God established the principle of government to maintain order. In resisting those in authority over us, we oppose the ordinance of God and will be accorded the consequences.

Protocols are in place to handle those who abuse their authority. Impeach, file a complaint, or contact superiors. Riots accomplish nothing but destruction.

Although David had been anointed king, he submitted to Saul's reign, waiting for the Lord's timing. His respect for Saul, a man who attempted to kill David several times, came from his love for God.

Lord, by submitting to the authority You have set in
place, we recognize and revere Your sovereignty.
Let those in power look to You for guidance.

ALWAYS THERE

The Lord is the Refuge and Stronghold of my life. . . .
Though a host encamp against me, my heart
shall not fear; though war arise against me,
[even then] in this will I be confident.
PSALM 27:1, 3 AMPC

Every woman wants a place where she can run and hide when things get tough. A place to reset, refuel, regain her composure before she says or does something she knows she'll regret. Of course, the woman who walks in the Way knows that place is in God, who is her stronghold. She knows He is always there waiting to help, to strengthen, to shower her with love, peace, joy, and confidence, to empower her to do all He's calling her to do.

How does she get there? By taking a mental and emotional pause. Delving deep within to find His presence, light, warmth, and assurance. Spending however much time she needs in that place. And then, and only then, moving forward in His name.

With You in my life, in my heart, I fear nothing.
You, Lord, are my all in all.

Day 24

TRUSTING THE MASTER PLANNER

*Blessed is the person who places his confidence in the
LORD and does not rely on arrogant people or those who
follow lies. You have done many miraculous things,
O LORD my God. You have made many wonderful
plans for us. No one compares to you!*
PSALM 40:4–5 GW

You've made a few plans, but it feels like it's taking forever for things to fall into place. You begin listening to others, finding yourself tempted to follow their advice. Before you know it, you're worrying, wringing your hands, wondering if you should try another tack or give up your plans altogether.

If you're not sure you're on the right path, share your concerns with the Master Planner. Place all your trust in Him, relying on His wisdom, for He's already done some marvelous things in your life. If your plans are aligned with His will and Word, you can rest easy. He'll give you the patience and peace you need to see things through—in His time and way.

*You have many wonderful plans for me, Lord.
I'm trusting You'll help me see them through.*

FEAR OF CONFRONTATION

*"Do not fear or be dismayed; tomorrow go out
to face them, for the LORD is with you."*
2 CHRONICLES 20:17 NASB

Intimidation has worked in the past. As a youngster, I cowered in fear when a raised voice was aimed at me. An angry stare would tongue-twist any clever comeback I might conjure up. My fear of confrontation followed me into adulthood until God reminded me that I'm not a doormat. I am His child.

In fear, Jehoshaphat sought the Lord's guidance and protection in the expected attack from his enemies. He proclaimed a nationwide fast, then glorified God before requesting His help.

Chapter 20 in 2 Chronicles gave me new confidence when faced with a dreaded confrontation. I give God the glory, then ask Him to strengthen, guide, and protect me.

Whether confronting a well-meaning friend, a bully, or a fierce enemy, let us turn to the Lord in prayer—first in praise, then in supplication.

*Lord God, we turn to You before facing
our enemies and pray for the right attitude
and words, as well as courage to confront
them with Christlike graciousness.*

Day 26

ANGELS NO STRANGERS

He will give His angels [especial] charge over you
to accompany and defend and preserve you in
all your ways [of obedience and service].
They shall bear you up on their hands.
PSALM 91:11–12 AMPC

Women are no strangers to angels. An angel found Hagar fleeing Sarah and told Hagar to go back and submit; she obeyed and her son became a leader of many nations. Angels rescued Lot's wife from God's wrath on Sodom but couldn't rescue her from looking back; when she gave in to her longing for the past, she became a pillar of salt. An angel appeared to Manoah's barren wife, telling her to take care of herself because she would soon be bearing a son. The angel Gabriel came to Mary, telling her that she was not to fear, the Lord was with her, *she'd* soon bear a son, and nothing was impossible with God! After Jesus' crucifixion, an angel told His female followers not to be afraid. Jesus lives! Rest easy and assured. God's angels are watching over you.

Thank You, Lord, for Your heavenly protection.

THE BIG ASK

"Ask and it will be given to you. Search and you will
find. Knock and the door will be opened for you.
The one who asks will always receive; the one who
is searching will always find, and the door is
opened to the man who knocks."
MATTHEW 7:7–8 PHILLIPS

In these days of information overload, your mind is likely overcluttered with various what-if scenarios swirling around in your head. It's likely that you're not even conscious of all these unchecked worries.

Fortunately, you have a Father God who can give you peace of mind, heart, spirit, and soul. As His daughter, you have the privilege to come before Him in prayer.

Jesus says that when you give God your worries and Ask for His peace, you'll get it. If you Seek the Father's presence, you'll find Him. If you Knock on the door of His home and love, He'll open it to you.

Ask, Seek, and Knock (ASK)—and be blessed with clarity, peace, and hope.

Here I am, Lord, giving, asking, seeking,
and knocking. Hear my prayer.

FEAR OF BEING VULNERABLE

So he said, "I heard Your voice in the garden, and I was afraid because I was naked; and I hid myself."
GENESIS 3:10 NKJV

Adam and Eve lost their innocence when they disobeyed God's only commandment to them. This left them vulnerable to new dangers in their environment, dangers that didn't exist before their sin transformed the world.

God used animal skins to protect them from exposure. A sacrificial lamb was the only way out of their predicament. This pointed toward our Father's ultimate solution of covering our sin with the blood of the Lamb, Jesus Christ.

Worldly circumstances thrust us into uncertainty. Alone in a stalled vehicle on a deserted road, a loved one in crisis, even various news reports make us feel weak and helpless. Unlike Adam and Eve, we are not naked. We are covered by His blood. Christ Jesus, who died for our sins, will always be with us. Let us call upon Him to come to our aid.

Gracious Lord, thank You for Your constant presence in our lives. Even when we feel alone, help us to remember You are here.

Day 29
COUNTER ACTS

"Oh, how my soul praises the Lord. How my spirit rejoices in God my Savior! For he took notice of his lowly servant girl. . . . For the Mighty One is holy, and he has done great things for me. . . . His mighty arm has done tremendous things!"

LUKE 1:46–49, 51 NLT

Studies have shown that keeping a gratitude journal reduces your stress! That's because people who count their blessings are more focused on how good things are. These "counter acts" naturally counteract stress, making blessing counters more resilient and more able to face whatever comes their way!

When was the last time you thanked God? What did you thank Him for? How can you make counting your blessings part of your regular routine?

Consider listing at least five things you're grateful for before going to bed at night. Doing so will not only make you a more optimistic, content, and joyful person, but it will help you sleep better!

Lord of my life, my heart rejoices in You as my lips thank You for. . .

PROOF OF THE PROMISE

And how bold and free we then become in his presence,
freely asking according to his will, sure that he's
listening. And if we're confident that he's listening,
we know that what we've asked for is as good as ours.
1 JOHN 5:14–15 MSG

In Mark 11:24, Jesus said that you'll get what you ask for if you really believe. Such a promise was proven by an account of a woman who'd been bleeding for twelve years. She'd been to lots of doctors and still was not whole. Hearing Jesus was coming, she sneaked up to Him, saying to herself, "If I only touch his garment, I will be made well" (Matthew 9:21 ESV). Jesus saw her and said, "Take heart, daughter; your faith has made you well" (Matthew 9:22 ESV). And in that instant, she was!

Take your concerns to God. Let Him know your desires. Then leave all in His hands, believing that He's listened and what you've asked for is already yours—and it will be.

Jesus, You prove the promises, so I'm bringing
You all my concerns, knowing what You
will for me is already mine.

COURAGE TO LIVE IN HARMONY

Now may the God of patience and comfort grant you to be like-minded toward one another, according to Christ Jesus, that you may with one mind and one mouth glorify the God and Father of our Lord Jesus Christ.
ROMANS 15:5–6 NKJV

An orchestra begins with a cacophony of instruments playing different tunes. To open their performance, the first chair violinist plays the *A* note. The other musicians then tune their instruments to that one note to reach the perfect blend of harmony.

God orchestrated His harmony in the Garden of Eden. Man brought dissonance when he rebelled against his Creator. Our heavenly Father played the perfect note in His Son, Jesus Christ. The best way to reach the precise balance of harmony with Him is by tuning our hearts to His Word.

We can find true harmony when we imitate Christ by putting others first. Accepting one another as Christ accepts us creates a soothing melody for life.

Father God, please grant us the courage to accept one another, to respond in one accord to Your perfect note, and to seek to live in harmony.

Day 32

A SIMPLE THING

"You will see neither wind nor rain. . .but this valley
will be filled with water. You will have plenty. . . .
But this is only a simple thing for the LORD,
for he will make you victorious."
2 KINGS 3:16–18 NLT

You're up against it, with no idea what to do. Nor any idea of
what God might do.

But here's the good news. God has a plan. One you cannot
even begin to imagine. The only thing you need to remember,
to rely on, is that what *seems* like an impossible task, an insurmountable problem, an unbelievable situation is nothing to
God. For Him, it's "only a simple thing." He's going to make
you victorious. Your role? To remind yourself that God is in
control and to trust Him to whom the solution is a simple thing.
"The next day. . .water suddenly appeared! . . . Soon there was
water everywhere" (2 Kings 3:20 NLT).

I know You're going to work it all out, Lord. So here
I am, leaving this "simple thing" in Your hands.

— Day 33 —
BECOMING A BLESSING

The LORD said to Abram, "Leave your land,
your relatives, and your father's home. Go to the land
that I will show you. I will make you a great nation,
I will bless you. I will make your name great,
and you will be a blessing."
GENESIS 12:1–2 GW

Chances are that most of your worries are about you and your own life, and that's only normal. But after you've come to God in prayer and dropped your worries off with Him, He would have you leave the land of You-ville behind and come into the land He'll show you—the one where it's all about God and others.

Freed up from your own concerns, you now have room and time to bring to God the concerns of others. That's you following Jesus and using the kingdom power of prayer on behalf of others. That's you becoming a blessing to others and God, continuing the work your Master started.

God's ready to go. Are you?

I have friends I'd like to bring to
You today, Abba. They need Your blessing.

COURAGE IN ANONYMITY

And I was unknown by face to the churches
of Judea which were in Christ.
GALATIANS 1:22 NKJV

We find safety in anonymity. When our sins aren't displayed in public, no one is the wiser to our humanity. That's why it's easier to tell strangers about Christ's love than our own family members. Those who knew us before we put our trust in Jesus would probably view us as hypocrites. They don't trust the change in our lives.

Paul must've been relieved that the churches of Judea didn't know him by sight. His earlier persecution of the Christians would have tainted his message. He could reach more people with the Gospel if they didn't know about his life before Christ blinded him on the road to Damascus. They might not have believed a radical transformation could've been possible for such a sinner saved by grace. Paul used his anonymity well.

Dear God, give us courage to offer the "unseen hand
of kindness" and bless others anonymously. May our
love for You be so evident that at least one stubborn
family member will follow in our footsteps.

COMMITTED SEAFARERS

Commit your actions to the Lord,
and your plans will succeed.
PROVERBS 16:3 NLT

The Roman philosopher Lucius Annaeus Seneca said, "If a man does not know to what port he is steering, no wind is favorable to him." That's enough to make a woman stop and think about her plans.

When we're not focused on where we think God wants us to go, we feel as if we're getting nowhere. This lack of direction can lead to stress, the stress a seafarer may feel when all she seems to be doing is wandering around the oceans, trying not to get shipwrecked by a storm, and feeling lost with no safe port in sight.

You know God has a purpose for your life. Be assured that as long as you put everything you're doing in His hands—leaving the results to Him and Him alone—not only will your stress abate, but God will make your plans succeed.

Lord, I'm looking to You to help me navigate these
waters. I commit all my plans and works to You.

GETTING A FAITH-LIFT

Anxiety in a man's heart weighs him down,
but a good word makes him glad.
PROVERBS 12:25 ESV

Worry is a weight that presses upon your heart. That's why the psalmist wrote that you should "Pile your troubles on GOD's shoulders—he'll carry your load, he'll help you out" (Psalm 55:22 MSG). That's why Jesus told you not to be anxious about anything but come to Him if you're heavy laden; that He'll give you the rest you need (see Matthew 6:25; 11:28–29). That's why Peter reminds you to "Give all your worries and cares to God, for he cares about you" (1 Peter 5:7 NLT).

But where's a modern woman to obtain that "good word" she needs to make her glad? In God's Word. Find a verse, psalm, or story that speaks to your heart. When you do, you'll find yourself lifted up to the heavenly God who waits to greet you.

My heart is heavy, Lord, so I'm digging into Your Word.
Reveal the words I need to lift me up to You.

Day 37

FEAR OF FAME

And the fame of David went out into all lands;
and the LORD brought the fear of him upon all nations.
1 CHRONICLES 14:17 KJV

Broadway and Hollywood are filled with young people seeking fame and fortune in the entertainment world. Athletes strive to be the most famous player on the team. But some of these fame-seekers fear how celebrity will affect their lives.

Public figures are media magnets. They have no privacy and their adoring fans put them on high pedestals and impose unrealistic expectations on them. Fame can bring pride and conceit, causing the fans to lose interest. The celebrity is no longer in demand.

King David's fame might have gone to his head. In his pride, he took many wives. But in humility, he consulted the Lord before every battle.

Although King David's reputation has endured thousands of years, most celebrities' fame today is fleeting. It only lasts one or two generations, and then they're forgotten like yesterday's newspaper.

What a blessing to know our Lord is a famous King forever.

King of kings, Lord of lords, Your fame
will endure to every generation.

Day 38

HANGING ON TIGHT

The minute I said, "I'm slipping, I'm falling," your love, GOD, took hold and held me fast. When I was upset and beside myself, you calmed me down and cheered me up.

PSALM 94:18–19 MSG

Nothing this week, month, year, has worked out right. No matter how hard you try, nothing seems to be going your way. You are not only stressed out but feeling helpless, as if you're falling and no one is waiting to catch you.

Tell God how you're feeling, how much pressure you're under, how alone and hopeless you feel. As soon as you do, He'll grab hold of you and hang on tight. He'll calm you down, open your eyes to the blessings around you, and put a smile back on your face.

What are you waiting for? Take advantage of the One who has chosen you and vowed to walk with you, to talk to you like a friend. The One who will never, ever let you go.

Jesus, I feel as if I'm slipping, falling.
Grab on to me. Never let me go.

— Day 39 —
CONFIDENCE IN GOD

*I know and rest in confidence upon it that the Lord
will maintain the cause of the afflicted, and will
secure justice for the poor and needy.*
PSALM 140:12 AMPC

According to headlines, evil and violence appear to be on the rise. Hearing all the bad news that's out there, you may find yourself worrying not only about your own safety but about the safety of others, as well as justice for the afflicted. It's almost too much to take in! Yet you weren't meant or designed to do so.

Your only recourse is to just hand those suffering over to God and to rest in the confidence that *He* will take care of all those harmed by evil and violence. That *He* will see justice for His children. It may not happen tomorrow, in your lifetime, or on this side of heaven, but it will happen. In God's time and way.

Meanwhile, begin lifting to God all those who are troubled, and leave the outcome in His hands.

*Lord, I'm handing over the afflicted to You.
Heal their hearts, and bring them justice.*

FEAR OF INSIGNIFICANCE

*"So do not fear; you are more
valuable than many sparrows."*
MATTHEW 10:31 NASB

Jesus sent forth His apostles as sheep in the midst of wolves to bear His message. A plentiful harvest of souls must have seemed insurmountable to the twelve men, giving them reason to fear their own irrelevance.

Like the apostles, we might fear our insignificance in the world system. I've suffered a near-anxiety attack while waiting hours in a long line for assistance. I feared no one cared about my needs. Was I a person, or merely a faceless number to a harried clerk? But then I remembered the sparrow.

God loves the little sparrow, a humble sacrifice for the poor who couldn't afford a lamb, and yet He values us more than that tiny bird. None of us are unimportant to our Creator. He knows how many hairs are on our heads and has a purpose for each of us.

*Lord God, remind us of the lowly sparrow when we
fear being insignificant, so we may remember
that You love us with an everlasting love.*

JUST BECAUSE

"Don't be afraid; you are more valuable to
God than a whole flock of sparrows."
MATTHEW 10:31 NLT

In the Bible, God consistently tells His people to be still, take a break from the everyday stress and strain, step out of this crazy world, and get to know Him (see Psalm 46:10). But it sometimes seems that before we can do this, we have to come to terms with the fact that God loves and values us just the way we are. Pastor and author Max Lucado puts it this way: "You are valuable because you exist. Not because of what you do or what you have done, but simply because you are."

Let your stress melt away as you spend some time in God's presence today with the knowledge there is nothing you must do to prove yourself to Him. You can have the greatest relationship with your Creator just by hanging with Him and knowing He loves you just because you're you.

Thank You, Lord, for loving me just the way I am.

BELIEVE AND LOOK

*[What, what would have become of me] had I not
believed that I would see the Lord's goodness in the land
of the living! Wait and hope for and expect the Lord;
be brave and of good courage. . . . Yes, wait for
and hope for and expect the Lord.*

PSALM 27:13–14 AMPC

The AMPC translation above asks what would become of you
if you didn't believe you'd see God's goodness in the world in
which you're now living. If you let your worries and anxieties
have complete sway over you, annihilating any hope that God
will do something and you *will* see the results.

God's Word puts it this way: "I believe that I shall look upon
the goodness of the LORD in the land of the living!" (Psalm
27:13 ESV). That's a simple verse to memorize, fortifying your
faith and giving you hope when all seems hopeless. Make it
part of your arsenal. Determine to look to God with complete
dependence and trust. Then you'll find the strength and courage
to get through anything.

*I expect to see Your goodness, Lord,
in this land. This gives me hope.*

FEAR OF REJECTION

He is despised and rejected of men;
a man of sorrows, and acquainted with grief.
ISAIAH 53:3 KJV

Rejection cuts like a knife through the heart.

A prospective employer offers the job to someone else.

Your valuable gift is callously dismissed.

Your spouse turns away from you.

Fear of being rejected prevents us from moving forward to seek a better job, other recipients for our gifts, or a possible reconciliation. For writers, rejection looms with every piece of work we submit. But we keep writing.

As Isaiah prophesied, many people still reject Jesus. Those who scorn Christ offer His work of salvation to their false gods. They callously refuse His precious gift of eternal life. They spurn the love that Jesus offers to His bride—the body of believers.

Jesus prayed, "Let this cup pass from me" (Matthew 26:39), yet He accepted God's will. He didn't permit any fear of rejection to thwart God's plan for salvation.

O Lord, give us courage in our fear of rejection.
Let us remember the man of sorrows, acquainted
with grief—our Christ, who will never
reject us because He first loved us.

REAP THE JOYS

*Let's see how inventive we can be in encouraging love
and helping out, not avoiding worshiping together
as some do but spurring each other on.*
HEBREWS 10:24–25 MSG

Stress can affect us in a variety of ways, including mentally, physically, and emotionally. One way to keep ourselves happy and healthy in all those areas is to connect with like-minded people, that is, other Christians. And what better way to do that than through church! Gather for worship with fellow believers. Find or found a ministry that feeds a passion in your own life. Perhaps a knitting and crocheting group that makes prayer shawls, a quilting group that makes blankets, a cooking group that helps at soup kitchens, a landscaping group that commits random acts of kindness in people's yards or along the highways.

Before you know it, you'll be distancing yourself from the fallow fields of stress and forging new ground where you can reap the joys of serving and encouraging others.

*Show me, Lord, what passion I can
pursue that can, at the same time,
serve others—in Your love and name!*

Day 45
GOD'S COMMAND FOR YOU

"This is my command—be strong and courageous!
Do not be afraid or discouraged. For the LORD
your God is with you wherever you go."
JOSHUA 1:9 NLT

Moses has died, and Joshua is left to lead God's people into the Promised Land. Can you imagine all the thoughts that must have been going through Joshua's head? Perhaps that's why God tells him three times to be strong and courageous and two times that He would be with him (see Joshua 1:5–9).

Chances are your challenges are not as great as Joshua's. But even if they are, these are the words God wants you to take to heart. Forget about worrying. That will only sap your energy and courage. Instead, know with certainty that God IS with you. He will NEVER leave you. No matter where you go, God is there. So be strong and brave. God's got you.

Thank You, Lord, for these encouraging words.
Help me get them through my head so that
I can be the strong and courageous
woman You've designed me to be!

Day 46

FEAR OF ACCEPTANCE

But in every nation whoever fears Him and
works righteousness is accepted by Him.
ACTS 10:35 NKJV

As we interview for a new position, which do we fear more—that they won't hire us, or that we'll get the job? Their offer means new responsibilities and, often, new coworkers, which might be scarier than being turned down for the job.

Acceptance by this world is threefold. It's usually based on proper behavior, pleasing appearance, and a positive attitude. One "off day" brings the anxiety that those who witnessed our angry outburst will no longer accept us. Is it any wonder we sometimes fear it?

Paul's persecution of the Christians before heading to Damascus was acceptable by his peers. Then he was beaten, stoned, and imprisoned by some of those same people for preaching the salvation of the Lord through Jesus Christ.

He chose God's acceptance over the world and encourages us to make that same choice. If we turn our fear of acceptance into fear of the Lord, then He will reckon it to us as righteousness.

Loving Father, thank You for
accepting us just as we are.

A GODLY GUFFAW

A cheerful disposition is good for your health;
gloom and doom leave you bone-tired.
PROVERBS 17:22 MSG

So many sources of news are vying for our attention. The anchorperson tells us war is in our midst or just over the horizon. The radio broadcasts the latest shooting. The meteorologist warns us of the next hurricane, drought, earthquake, flood, or snowstorm. The newspaper reports the latest police news. The cell phone updates the terrorist level. The neighbor reports on the breakup of the couple around the corner. Before we know it, we're suffocating under a barrage of bad news.

Take a break. Put the TV on mute. Shut off the radio. Forget about the weather. Recycle the paper. Power down your phone. Shut your front door. And watch a comedy show or movie that gives you genuine belly laughs. Allow God's gift of laughter to heal you, to lift you out of your stress and into His holy joy. Get yourself a godly guffaw!

Lord, I'm stuck in a bad-news rut.
Help me hone in on Your healing joy.

THORNS OF WORRY AND RICHES

"The seed planted among thornbushes is another person who hears the word. But the worries of life and the deceitful pleasures of riches choke the word so that it can't produce anything."

MATTHEW 13:22 GW

Jesus tells a parable about a farmer who sows seed. The seed that fell on the path is grabbed up by birds (the evil one). The seed sown on the rocky ground quickly withers when the sun scorches it. These are people of little faith who lost their way when troubles came. The seeds that fell amid thorns got choked out. These are people who allowed the cares of the world and money to choke God's Word out of their life, making them unfruitful.

Your goal is to give your worries to God. Do not focus on the treasures of this world. Grow on God's Word, allowing it to build you up. Then you'll be the fruitful seed, yielding more crops than you ever thought possible.

God's waiting. Bloom where He's planted you.

Help me bear fruit for You, Lord, as I let go of my worries and take up Your Word.

Day 49
FEAR OF ABANDONMENT

*At my first defense no one supported me, but all
deserted me; may it not be counted against them.*
2 TIMOTHY 4:16 NASB

When someone we love abandons us, we might turn so far
inward that it's difficult to find the way out. But putting our
trust in Christ will give us courage to close that yawning pit
of despair before we fall into it. God has given us the choice
to either feel abandoned in a crowded room, or cheerful in an
empty house.

The world Jesus came to save abandoned Him. Paul's helpers
in Asia left him to preach by himself. Jesus asked God to forgive
those who crucified Him. Paul prayed that it not be counted
against those who deserted him. Can we emulate Jesus and
Paul when others forsake us? Healing begins with forgiveness.

People will abandon us, because we are all flawed sinners
saved by grace. But the Lord won't desert us. He is only a
prayer away.

*O Lord our God, we take comfort in Your promise
that You will not abandon Your people,
nor will You forsake Your inheritance.*

Day 50
FAITH, LOVE, AND HOPE

*We give thanks to God always for all of you, constantly
mentioning you in our prayers, remembering before our
God and Father your work of faith and labor of love
and steadfastness of hope in our Lord Jesus Christ.*
1 THESSALONIANS 1:2–3 ESV

The prayers of those who have gone before us are continually
before God (see Revelation 5:8; 8:3). *And* the prayers of our
loved ones stick to us like gum on a hot sidewalk. As Abraham
Lincoln said, "I remember my mother's prayers and they have
always followed me. They have clung to me all my life."

Not only do you have the prayer power to cover your own
loved ones, but saints, such as the apostle Paul, have used their
prayer power to cover *you*. Be encouraged by this. Know that
because of your faith, great things are happening and will happen in your life. That others are grateful for your labors in love.

Relax and tap into the timelessness of faith, love, and hope.

*Thank You, Jesus, for the faith, love,
and hope with which You bless me.*

GOD'S PATHWAY FOR YOU

*Your road led through the sea, your pathway through
the mighty waters—a pathway no one knew was there!
You led your people along that road like a flock of sheep,
with Moses and Aaron as their shepherds.*

PSALM 77:19–20 NLT

Worries may come upon you like mighty waters. Once you were standing in the shallows, then you wandered deeper into the depths, and before you knew it, you were caught in the undertow. How would you ever regain your footing?

Before you let your worries pull you under, go to God. Ask Him to show you the pathway you cannot see with your limited vision. He will clearly reveal the road He's carved out just for you, the path He's provided by dividing waters, obliterating the worry and despair that blocks your way. Then He'll calm you, take you by the hand, and carefully and masterfully guide you as any good and loving shepherd would.

*I don't want these worries to take me under, Lord.
Calm my soul. Take my hand. Lead me,
Good Shepherd, to safety and hope.*

Day 52

FEAR OF BEING OUTNUMBERED

But the LORD said to him, "Surely I will be with you,
and you shall defeat Midian as one man."
JUDGES 6:16 NASB

God promoted Gideon from farm boy to general of the Israelite army. When he enlisted thirty-two thousand soldiers, the Midianites outnumbered them four to one.

The Lord scaled back the unit letting twenty-two thousand men depart. Ten thousand were still too many, so He downsized again by testing their vigilance. With three hundred men remaining, they were outnumbered four hundred and fifty to one.

They went up on the mountain, each armed only with a trumpet and a clay jar holding a torch inside. Gideon signaled them to blow the trumpets, break the jars, and raise the torches. The Midianites fled.

Our concern isn't how powerful we are, but how powerful God is. When tears come, when disappointment is our friend, when our future looks bleak, when crushing circumstances paralyze us, fear not, for Jesus is with us. Holding tight to that promise, we can face any fear.

Omnipotent Father, we glorify You. We are never
outnumbered when You are with us.

Day 53
STRAIGHTEN UP

For God is not a God of disorder but of peace.
1 Corinthians 14:33 nlt

You have a commitment on Saturday, a birthday party for a little one. You have the gift, the gift bag, and the card but can't find the invitation. You're too embarrassed to call the hostess and ask what time you're supposed to show up. So you spend three days tearing your house apart. You finally call another friend who's going, hoping she hasn't lost *her* invitation. She hasn't. She gives you the show-up time and you do just that. The following Monday, you find your invitation under a pile of papers on your desk. Argh!

Has this, or something similar, ever happened to you? If so, it's time to straighten up your purse, desk, office, house. Doing so will keep you from suffering from disorderly stress and open up your days with some orderly peace.

Help me, Lord, to stop and straighten up my life
every once in a while. I know doing so will be
time spent in a worthy pursuit of peace.

Day 54

AT HOME IN GOD

You've taken my hand. You wisely and tenderly lead me,
and then you bless me. . . . I'm in the very presence
of God—oh, how refreshing it is! I've
made Lord GOD my home.
PSALM 73:23–24, 28 MSG

When you worry you'll never find your way, take a look at where you're standing. Have you moved away from God?

Remember the Lord is your rock, fortress, and shelter. When you get close to Him in prayer, He'll take your hand and lead you exactly where you need to go, and then He'll bless you as soon as your feet touch down on the path He's opened up for you.

Today, get yourself into the presence of God. Allow Him to take your hand. As you do, you'll not only find the refreshment you've been thirsting for but the home your spirit and soul have been longing for—in Him alone.

Lord, when doubts and worries assail me,
help me get back to You, my only true
home in this world and the next.

Day 55

FEAR OF GOOD NEWS

And the angel said unto them, Fear not:
for, behold, I bring you good tidings of
great joy, which shall be to all people.
LUKE 2:10 KJV

The shepherds watching their flock that night thought their evening would be like any other. Lying in the grass, gazing up at the sky. The stars must've been bright in the darkness. Only the occasional bleating of sheep disturbed the quiet in the field.

Then the angel appeared, and the glory of the Lord lit up the pasture.

Good news means change. Jesus' birth radically transformed how people would relate to God. The religious leaders of that day were comfortable in their ritualistic traditions. They rejected this strange good news.

After Jesus' death and resurrection, Luke recorded the uprising in Ephesus. Paul's good news changed hearts, and Demetrius, who produced silver shrines to the Greek goddess Artemis, lost a large amount of business.

Who is your Demetrius, contented in traditions and rejecting your good news?

O Lord our God, give us the courage to
continue sharing the good tidings of great
joy offered two thousand years ago.

SEE THE TREES

Ask the birds of the air, and let them tell you; or speak to the earth [with its many forms of life], and it will teach you; and let the fish of the sea declare [this truth] to you.

JOB 12:7–8 AMP

God wants you out and about, looking at His creation, learning its lessons, breathing in its beauty, praising its presence, allowing it to speak. Amazingly enough, looking at trees—the more the better—will relieve your stress! Both exercising amid the boughs and just looking at them will lower your blood pressure and lift your mood. What an amazing God you have, who has given you a simple way to lower your stress.

Whether you live in the city or the country, find a tree or three or more. Beat a path to a forest floor. Or simply stare at some trees from your window. Take a few deep belly breaths. Praise God for the trees' beauty and power to lift your spirits. See the trees and ease the stress.

Thank You, Lord, for the tranquility of Your trees.

GOD HAS A FIRM GRIP ON YOU

"Don't panic. I'm with you. There's no need to fear
for I'm your God. I'll give you strength. I'll help you.
I'll hold you steady, keep a firm grip on you.
Count on it: Everyone who had it in for you
will end up out in the cold—real losers."
ISAIAH 41:10–11 MSG

Isaiah 41:10–13 are wonderful verses to take hold of when worry turns to fear and then panic. They are words spoken by your God, who knows all things that have happened, are happening, and will happen to you.

God tells you not to panic because He is with you. He'll give you all the strength you need to face whatever lies before you. He has your hand, and He'll never let you go. He'll keep you steady on your feet, give you firm footing to walk where He'd have you go. And those who threaten you today will be gone tomorrow.

Believe, and you will have the strength and peace your heart, spirit, and soul crave.

Lord, in You I find my courage.
I'm counting on You alone!

COURAGE TO DELIVER BAD NEWS

And the servants of David were afraid
to tell him that the child was dead.
2 Samuel 12:18 nasb

No one wants to be the bearer of bad news. Are we more afraid of hurt feelings, or of their response? Will they quietly weep or tear the room apart in violent outrage?

Sometimes they surprise us, as David did his servants. David fasted and wept while his son was sick, praying that the child might live. When he learned his child had died, he got up and dressed. Knowing he would see his son in heaven, he was able to move forward. Psalm 112:7 states that a righteous man shall not be afraid of evil tidings. His heart is fixed, trusting in the Lord.

It's far more kind to deliver sad tidings quickly with gentleness than to wait for the right moment. There is no good time for bad news. We can remind them to fix their hearts in righteousness, trust in the Lord, and welcome His embrace.

Give us the courage and the right words, O God,
to bring comfort when delivering bad news.

ARE YOU THERE?

Let us also lay aside every weight. . .looking to Jesus,
the founder and perfecter of our faith.
HEBREWS 12:1–2 ESV

During Jesus' time on earth, no matter what was happening in His life, no matter how many people were vying for His attention, He kept His eyes on His Father. He went alone to a quiet place where He could get calm, focus, and spend time in the company of the Master Creator. This time of solitude and single-minded devotion allowed Him to come away refreshed, rejuvenated, replenished, ready to give His entire attention to those who came to Him.

Are you there for Jesus? Are you there for God? Are you there for others? Are you even there for yourself?

Unplug yourself from the world—including your phone, computer, TV, and radio—a few times a week, at least. Plug into God, Jesus, the Spirit. Spend time with the Creator and His creation. Then use that energy and power to plug into yourself and those around you. Focus, be fed, then feed. Be there.

Lord, help me to be there for You, myself, and others.
Be the reigning power in my life once again!

GOD TO THE RESCUE

*Though I am surrounded by troubles, you will protect
me from the anger of my enemies. You reach out your
hand, and the power of your right hand saves me.
The LORD will work out his plans for my life—
for your faithful love, O LORD, endures forever.*
PSALM 138:7–8 NLT

Sometimes life can surprise you. You're going along your merry way, and then all of a sudden, before you know it, you're surrounded by trouble. You're in the thick of a situation you never saw coming. Now you're more than worried—you're ready to freak out!

Stop. Take a deep breath no matter where you are or what you're doing. Remind yourself that God will—*is*—protecting you. His power is saving you in that very moment. He's going to work everything out for you. Why? Because He not only loves you but has a good plan for your life. All you need to do is trust Him and live it!

*Protect me, Lord, when danger steals in.
I know You'll save me. You have a plan!*

Day 61

FEAR OF CHANGE

*Behold, I tell you a mystery: We shall not
all sleep, but we shall all be changed.*
1 Corinthians 15:51 nkjv

Life-changing moments begin before our birth. We grow from a zygote to a baby in thirty-six weeks, developing muscular, skeletal, and nervous systems, blood vessels, organs, and tiny fingers and toes. Change continues rapidly on this side of the womb too. We learn to walk and talk, move from a liquid diet to solids, and grow in stature.

So why do some of us fear change? It often means letting go of our comfort zone and the familiar people, places, and things we've come to treasure. Yet our joy increases as we move forward in the newness of life.

While the world is in an uproar, we eagerly await the trumpet. Our light at the end of the tunnel will be Christ in His glory as He returns in the sky to take us with Him.

*Gracious Father, thank You for giving us hope
in the change to come. As we change from
mortal to immortal, we will be united
with You to enjoy our heavenly home.*

LET LOOSE

David was dancing before the LORD with great enthusiasm. . . . So David and all the house of Israel were bringing the ark of the LORD up [to the City of David] with shouts [of joy] and with the sound of the trumpet.

2 SAMUEL 6:14–15 AMP

There's a time to dance—either before, during, or after stressful situations. Try it. Why? Because dancing helps to de-stress you. Regardless of how well you do it, dancing releases endorphins, which make your body feel better and improve your mind's outlook, making you feel calmer and more optimistic. Even better is the fact that music, whether you're playing, dancing to, or listening to it, lowers pulse and heart rates, blood pressure, and stress hormone levels.

So let loose. Dance before the Lord. Praise Him with music and song. Pick up an instrument and play for Him. Before you know it, you'll be bringing joy to God and yourself!

I am so grateful for the power of music, Lord. Let's dance!

CONFESS AND REFRESH

*So repent (change your mind and purpose); turn
around and return [to God], that your sins may be
erased (blotted out, wiped clean), that times of refreshing
(of recovering from the effects of heat, of reviving with
fresh air) may come from the presence of the Lord.*

ACTS 3:19 AMPC

If handing your worries over to God in prayer isn't bringing
you peace, it may be you haven't told Him all that's been going
on in your life. You haven't confessed those things you don't
even want to admit to yourself. And so, they remain hidden
within you, festering like an unclean wound.

Dear woman, nothing is hidden from God. He sees all
you do, hears all you say (see Job 34:21). But if you want to
be refreshed, to have less worry and more peace, ask God
to examine you, to reveal the hidden missteps you have yet
to confess (see Psalm 139:23–24). Know that God *will* forgive you. And afterward you'll come away more refreshed
than ever!

*Lord, look within me. Reveal the misstep that's
keeping me anxious. Help me tell You all.*

Day 64
FEAR OF LIFE'S RUTS

Jesus Christ the same yesterday, and to day, and for ever.
HEBREWS 13:8 KJV

We take the same route to work every day, eat the same turkey sandwich for lunch, work on the same humdrum paperwork, and then take the same route home again. Our schedule has become a rut, and we begin to dread the sameness of our dull, drab lives. But we don't dare change anything that might affect our time line. That's when our fear of ruts becomes a phobia. We have the knowledge to mix up the schedule, but not the courage.

While our lives appear to be static, changes take place every day. The traffic flow to and from work changes, depending on light cycles. The bread slices have a different shape than the sandwich we ate the day before.

As we look at the sameness of life, we see hints of changes. That's because only One is unchanging—Jesus Christ, our eternal Savior.

Father in heaven, when we get caught up in our ruts of life, prompt us to make changes that remind us of Your timeless love.

BRINGING OUT THE BEST

*"I'm telling you to love your enemies. Let them bring
out the best in you, not the worst. When someone gives
you a hard time, respond with the supple moves of
prayer, for then you are working out of your
true selves, your God-created selves."*
MATTHEW 5:44–45 MSG

There are those authorities who tell you to stay away from
people who frustrate you, who stress you out. But Jesus tells
you to pray for them. To love them.

Inspirational writer William Arthur Ward has a wonderful
maxim to live by: "When we seek to discover the best in others,
we somehow bring out the best in ourselves."

Keep these thoughts in mind the next time you come
across a relative or acquaintance, a coworker or fellow church
member who brings out the fight, flight, or freeze response in
you. Look for the best in that person. And see what happens
within your own self.

*Lord, help me to continually love and look
for the best in everyone, as You do me.*

HABITUAL PRAYER

*Be earnest and unwearied and steadfast in your
prayer [life], being [both] alert and intent
in [your praying] with thanksgiving.*
COLOSSIANS 4:2 AMPC

If your prayer life is sporadic, so will your peace be. And if you
don't pepper your petitions with thanksgiving, your prayers will
become a mere litany of selfish desires you'd like fulfilled before
you go on your way and in your own power.

That's why the apostle Paul, the author of Colossians, encourages you to pray continually from the heart and to make
prayer a tireless habit in your life.

So don't go to God just once a day but throughout your day.
When you see someone suffering, pray. When worry begins to
creep into your mind, pray. While you're with God in all ways
all day, thank Him for all He has done, is doing, and will do.
In so doing, not only will all your worries fade, but you'll find
yourself walking God's way and in His power.

*Help me, Lord, to be steadfast in my prayer life,
continually giving thanks to You
in all ways all day.*

FEAR OF COMPETITION

*In a race everyone runs, but only one person
gets first prize. So run your race to win.*
1 CORINTHIANS 9:24 TLB

Whether in business, politics, or sports, competition reveals to us—and to our rivals—how proficient or deficient we are at a specific talent. When we're pitted against one whose ability seems far superior to ours, self-doubt attempts to trample our confidence. We don't give up mentally before we get started physically. We need to compete to grow and improve.

Competition compels us to diligently focus on self-discipline. As Christians, our race isn't against other humans, but against the adversary. Every lap and every hurdle represents our quest to win souls for Christ. God gave each of us a special talent to use for His glory. Some have a ministry of music, acting, or artwork. Others preach or write. We might not win an earthly, perishable prize, but our gold medal is waiting in heaven as we trounce the competition.

*God our Father, we won't slow down or stop
until we've run this race with endurance
to win and crossed Your finish line.*

Day 68
GO DEEP

Why are you in despair, O my soul? And why have you become restless and disturbed within me? Hope in God and wait expectantly for Him, for I shall again praise Him for the help of His presence.
PSALM 42:5 AMP

What do you do when moments of stress come on suddenly and there's nowhere to run and hide?

It's in those moments you need to recognize that all you're doing is facing a moment of stress. There's no real immediate danger. Take a deep breath and remember that God has promised never to leave you or forsake you. Although you don't have a physical quiet place to retreat to, you can meet God in the quiet place of your heart. Allow your spirit to go deep, to call to and be answered by the Holy Spirit within. Know His song is with you.

Help me to practice going deep with You, Lord, so I'll react with peace in You—within and without—no matter where I am.

Day 69

A STACK OF BLESSINGS WAITING FOR YOU

Desperate, I throw myself on you: you are my God!
Hour by hour I place my days in your hand. . . .
What a stack of blessing you have piled up for
those who worship you, ready and waiting for
all who run to you to escape an unkind world.
PSALM 31:14–15, 19 MSG

One good way to throw off worry is to throw yourself on God in the midst of it. Second by second, minute by minute, hour by hour, put yourself into the hands of the One who loves and protects you. The One who longs to talk to you, walk with you, and carry you when necessary.

No matter what your troubles or worries, God will find a unique way of making good come out of anything and everything that comes your way. So escape into God, knowing He has a stack of blessings waiting just for you.

My worries evaporate when I put myself
in Your hands, Lord. In You a stack of
blessings are waiting—just for me!

COURAGE TO FACE THE FUTURE

" 'For I know the plans that I have for you,'
declares the LORD, 'plans for welfare and not for
calamity to give you a future and a hope.' "
JEREMIAH 29:11 NASB

The future of our nation looks bleak. The moral compass is spinning, searching for the point of legitimacy buried in sin long ago. Our leaders call evil good, and good evil. Do we fret in despair, or carry on in prayer?

The godly men and women of thirteen colonies considered their future dismal too. Yet with God's help, a mighty nation grew out of their bravery and sacrifice. They sowed the seeds of hope for future generations. If we plant the seeds of the Gospel of Jesus Christ, then those who follow us will find a harvest of hope.

Is our world falling apart, or falling into place? God knows the plans He has for us, for our nation, and the world. He tells us His plans in His Word.

Dear Lord, we've read the end of the Bible.
Knowing Your victory over evil encourages
us to face our futures with hope.

DECISIONS, DECISIONS

*Such things were written in the Scriptures long
ago to teach us. And the Scriptures give us hope
and encouragement as we wait patiently for
God's promises to be fulfilled.*
ROMANS 15:4 NLT

Even the easiest of decisions can seem difficult at times, especially when many different choices are available to us. So what's a woman to do to receive good and godly guidance every day?

Spend time with God, an open Bible upon your lap. Before reading the scriptures, let your prayer be something like this:

*Lord, tell me what You want me to know.
Show me what You want me to see.
Lead me where You want me to go.
Make me what You want me to be.*

Then rest assured that God will give you the wisdom to make the right decision in His eyes.

*I know You will give me all the wisdom I desire,
Lord. Walk with me. Talk to me. I await Your
direction with patience and trust.*

GOD'S GATEWAY OF HOPE

"I will lead her into the desert and speak tenderly to her there. I will return her vineyards to her and transform the Valley of Trouble into a gateway of hope."

HOSEA 2:14–15 NLT

God is so tenderhearted toward you. He desires to spend time with you, to speak to you. So go to Him with your worries. Pour out all the anxious thoughts in your mind. Unburden your heart of all that's concerning you. Tell Him everything that's troubling your spirit and keeping you from focusing on Him.

As you do so, God will come close and listen. Then He will talk to you with a soft voice, pour out His wisdom, and cover you with His love. He will bless you with His peace and presence. Before you know it, you'll find Him transforming your dark valley of despair into a shining gateway of hope.

Lord, I feel lost in this dark Valley of Trouble. So I come to You, pouring out my heart. Lead me to the gateway of the hope I have in You!

COURAGE TO TRUST THE LORD

But the centurion said, "Lord, I am not worthy
for You to come under my roof, but just say the
word, and my servant will be healed."
MATTHEW 8:8 NASB

A centurion commanded a hundred Roman soldiers. They were zealous because they feared him more than the enemy.

Compassion, not fierceness, brought the centurion of Capernaum to Jesus. We can learn much from his brief encounter.

He approached the Lord with concern for his servant's well-being. God wants us to love one another and look out for each other in this way.

He cited his own unworthiness. God's Word tells us a man's pride will bring him low, but a humble spirit will obtain honor.

He trusted Jesus at His word. To say in prayer, "Just say the word," shows faith in God's heartfelt compassion when we don't see His hand working in our lives.

He acknowledged Jesus' divine authority. Just as God spoke the world into existence, Jesus can speak healing into a paralytic.

O God, whose Word I praise, send forth Your
loving-kindness and Your truth. Give us the courage
to trust You enough to pray, "Just say the word."

CAUGHT UP

*Simon answered, "Master, we toiled all night and took
nothing! But at your word I will let down the nets."
And when they had done this, they enclosed a large
number of fish, and their nets were breaking.*
LUKE 5:5–6 ESV

Sometimes we get so caught up in our lives, so stressed out,
that we don't recognize where God may be directing our attention, the solutions He might be providing if only we'd look or
listen, whether through circumstances, prayer, the wisdom of
others, or the scriptures.

Consider how Jesus was preaching one day from Simon's
boat after a long night of unsuccessful fishing on the part of
Simon and his crew. Yet at Jesus' word, Simon lowered his
nets—and brought up a bounty of fish.

Are you awake and open to what God is saying? Where
might He be telling you to let down your net?

*Lord, I come before You, my eyes and ears open.
What would You have me do?*

YOUR WORRY LIST

Keep your life free from love of money, and be content
with what you have, for he has said, "I will never
leave you nor forsake you." So we can confidently say,
"The Lord is my helper; I will not fear."
HEBREWS 13:5–6 ESV

Someone once wrote, "You can tell the size of your God by looking at the size of your worry list. The longer your list, the smaller your God." Hm. How big is *your* God? How long is *your* worry list?

Do your concerns revolve around money or things you don't really need? Is your discontent rising up because you don't have the latest cell phone, the most fashionable clothes, the best-looking lawn, or the nicest car?

Today consider writing down your worries. See how many things you can cross off, knowing you can be content with what you have. Then hand over to God whatever worries are left, trusting Him, your helper, to provide whatever you truly need.

Lord, help me be content with what I have and
trust You to provide all things I truly do need.

FEAR OF SEPARATION

*For perhaps he was for this reason separated from you
for a while, that you would have him back forever.*
PHILEMON 1:15 NASB

Children grow up and leave for college or a career. Friends relocate for marriage or work. Death takes a spouse, a sibling, or a parent. Separation takes many forms. Most are difficult to accept, but nothing is worse than separation from God. Adam and Eve suffered that fate when, due to their rebellion, God expelled them from the presence of His love. We've been trying to find our way back since the Fall. God provided the Way—Jesus.

Onesimus ran away as a slave, but returned as a brother in Christ. Paul petitioned Philemon to forgive Onesimus's defiance and offered to pay the debt the former slave owed.

Like Philemon's slave, we ran away from God, defiantly seeking our own way. Christ rescued us; paid the outstanding debt we owed, and returned us as coheirs to the kingdom.

*God our Father, circumstances separate us from our
loved ones, but nothing will separate us from
Your love through Christ Jesus.*

PATIENTLY PONDER IN PRAYER

Mary was keeping within herself all these things
(sayings), weighing and pondering them in her heart.
LUKE 2:19 AMPC

Events you never foresaw are happening all around you. There is so much going on, so much commotion in your world and life that your thoughts are pitter-pattering like so many raindrops splashing onto a tin roof. You begin losing sleep in the night hours, wondering what will happen next or how you can keep what you *think* is going to happen from happening. In the daytime, your judgment becomes skewed. You have so many thoughts careening around in your head, you can no longer take information in.

What's missing in your life? Patiently pondering in prayer, trusting that God is with you and will reveal things in His own good time. As Mother Teresa said, "Prayer is not asking. Prayer is putting oneself in the hands of God, at His disposition, and listening to His voice in the depths of our hearts."

Lord, help me to pray, ponder, and put myself
in Your hands as You speak to my heart.

OPEN DOORS

*"Behold, I have set before you an open door,
which no one is able to shut. I know that you
have but little power, and yet you have kept
my word and have not denied my name."*

REVELATION 3:8 ESV

Ever worry that you might be on the wrong path? Have you had a door opened or shut in your face lately? No need to worry. As Catherine Wood Marshall wrote, "Often God has to shut a door in our face so that He can subsequently open the door through which He wants us to go."

God has a definite plan for your life. He wants you to be successful, to prosper, to bloom where He's planted you. So instead of worrying if you're on the right or wrong road, go to God. Ask Him to come up behind you and tell you which way to turn, if turn you must. Rest easy, knowing He's guiding you and won't let you go down any rabbit holes.

*Lord, show me what doors You've opened—or shut.
I'm trusting You to lead me the right way.*

THE COURAGE TO ASK

*Joseph of Arimathea came, a prominent member of
the Council, who himself was waiting for the kingdom
of God; and he gathered up courage and went in
before Pilate, and asked for the body of Jesus.*

MARK 15:43 NASB

Abraham mustered the courage to ask God to spare Sodom
and Gomorrah, bartering down to ten righteous people. The
Lord answered each plea with a yes.

Joseph of Arimathea, fearful of his fellow Jews, had to gather
up courage to request Jesus' body for burial.

Each man asked for favor that matched God's will. God
would have spared Sodom and Gomorrah if only He had found
ten righteous men there. Pilate unknowingly fulfilled the details
of Jesus' burial foretold by the prophet Isaiah.

We have no need to fear asking anything of the Lord, if
we ask it in Christ's name. For in His name is God's will. Jesus
said, "For everyone who asks receives, and he who seeks finds,
and to him who knocks it will be opened" (Matthew 7:8).

*Gracious Father, thank You for allowing
us to boldly come to Your throne of
glory with our petitions.*

REST VERSUS STRESS

Stand by the roads and look; and ask for the eternal paths, where the good, old way is; then walk in it, and you will find rest for your souls. But they said, We will not walk in it!

JEREMIAH 6:16 AMPC

Have a decision to make? A path to choose? Looking for direction? For peace? God has all the answers for you and even outlines them in Jeremiah 6:16. Step 1: Stand where you are and look around. Consider all the possible options. Step 2: Pray. Ask God for His good way. Step 3: Walk in it. Now that you know the right way (through praying for wisdom, heeding God's voice, and using the Bible as your road map), you will find rest for your soul.

You could also choose (a) to do none of those things or (b) to refuse to walk in the path God has laid out for you. Both of those options lead to stress.

So stop. Stand by, now, in this moment. Take steps 1 through 3. Choose rest, not stress.

I'm at the crossroads, Lord, looking for Your way.

IT'S *GOD* WHO SAVES

*The LORD said to Gideon, "You have too many warriors
with you. If I let all of you fight the Midianites,
the Israelites will boast to me that they saved
themselves by their own strength."*

JUDGES 7:2 NLT

God told Gideon to gather an army to defeat the Midianites, who'd been raiding Israel. But Gideon had too many warriors with him, so many that the Israelites might imagine their own strength had saved them instead of God.

So, through a series of commands to Gideon, God pared down his army from thirty-two thousand to three hundred men, who went on to defeat their enemy.

It's plain to see that when God is in your camp, you need not worry you don't have enough resources to win the day. God will equip you with all the strength, power, and provisions you need—for the victory lies solely in *His* hands!

*All I need to win the day is to have You on my side,
Lord. You'll provide me with all the strength,
power, and provisions I need because the
victory is in Your hands alone!*

Day 82

COURAGE TO BE APPRAISED

If any man's work which he has built on it remains, he will receive a reward. If any man's work is burned up, he will suffer loss; but he himself will be saved, yet so as through fire.

1 Corinthians 3:14–15 nasb

Fear of exams changes our study habits. Hoping for more than just a passing grade, we pay closer attention to the teacher, then read and reread the text until we're comfortable with the course material.

In the workforce, fear of job loss or no pay increase drives us to improve our professional behavior for an upcoming job evaluation. We make punctuality a priority, double-check our work, and put on a happy face for our coworkers and managers.

As God's people, we face a future heavenly appraisal. Not a judgment of condemnation, but of rewards. The decisions we make today will determine how well we fare before God's bema seat. Will we present Him with works of wood, hay, and straw or gold, silver, and precious gems?

Merciful Father, keep us ever mindful of the impact our decisions today make on our eternity with You in heaven.

PERCEPTION

The LORD said to Samuel, "Don't judge by his appearance or height, for I have rejected him. The LORD doesn't see things the way you see them. People judge by outward appearance, but the LORD looks at the heart."

1 SAMUEL 16:7 NLT

Stress often comes to the fore when we think we need to and *do* have all the answers. When we think that what we perceive is indeed the true and only reality. But God turns that idea upside down over and over in the Bible, perhaps most notably when the prophet Samuel looked to secretly anoint one of Jesse's eight sons as the next king. He began with the oldest and ended up with David, the youngest and smallest of Jesse's boys. Selecting him went against all logic, all human sense and reasoning. But Samuel obeyed.

God sees so much more than you do. Your role is to seek His knowledge, let Him have His say, then do as He wills, regardless of how much sense it makes to you.

Help me, Lord, to seek and be open to Your vision in every situation I face.

LIKE A CHILD

But Jesus said, "Let the children come to me.
Don't stop them! For the Kingdom of Heaven
belongs to those who are like these children."
MATTHEW 19:14 NLT

Little children don't worry. That's because they trust in their parents for everything—food, clothing, water, protection, and love. They're vulnerable and cannot get far without their mother's or father's help and guidance. So they're happy to take their parent's hand, knowing they'll be safely led across the street, through the store, or up the stairs to bed.

That's how God wants you to be—like a trusting child. He wants you not to worry about anything but to rely on Him for everything. He wants you to be humble, realizing your complete dependence upon Him, knowing you won't get far without your hand in His.

Be like a child and you'll find yourself growing up securely in God.

You are such a good father and mother to me, Lord.
Help me be like a little child, realizing You'll
safely lead me where You'd have me go.
I'm putting myself in Your hands.

Day 85

COURAGE TO FACE THE TRUTH

*"And you will know the truth,
and the truth will make you free."*
JOHN 8:32 NASB

The truth hurts only if we don't want to hear it. If I have parsley stuck in my teeth, it isn't painful for someone to let me know. If a loved one is seriously ill, the truth of the diagnosis and treatment can hurt deeply. But knowing the truth opens doors and sets us free for more choices and opportunities.

The Jewish authorities Jesus spoke to did not want to hear His truth. They asserted their lineage to Abraham and, since they hadn't been enslaved, questioned His comment about being free. Their claim to be free from sin was nullified by their murderous thoughts toward Jesus.

God's truth hurts when we first give up a sinful lifestyle. The pain of surrendering our enslaved minds and hearts is soon replaced by the healing freedom in Christ Jesus. That new freedom gives us the courage to face the truth.

*Righteous Father, thank You for giving us freedom
in the divine revelation of Your truth.*

GOD'S OWN HEART

"God removed Saul and replaced him with David,
a man about whom God said, 'I have found David
son of Jesse, a man after my own heart. He will
do everything I want him to do.' "
ACTS 13:22 NLT

So many rules are out there. And they've been around for years. Look at all the rules the Pharisees made and insisted the Jews follow. Trying to follow them was most likely unbelievably stressful.

Fortunately, God makes things simple for those who follow Christ. He wants you to be a *God*-follower more than just a *rule*-follower. All you have to do is listen and obey. Make His will yours. You can begin by loving God with all your heart, mind, body, spirit, soul, and strength. And then love others as yourself.

Let the stress and unnecessary rules fall away. Become a woman after God's own heart.

Lord, help me be a woman who follows the
Rule Giver more than the rules. Help me
be a woman after Your own heart.

STAND STILL AND SEE

Be not afraid or dismayed at this great multitude;
for the battle is not yours, but God's. . . . You shall not
need to fight in this battle; take your positions, stand still,
and see the deliverance of the Lord [Who is] with you.
2 CHRONICLES 20:15, 17 AMPC

After King Jehoshaphat prayed, God told the king and his people not to worry or be dismayed because the battle before them was God's. All they were to do was to go where God told them to go, stand there, and watch Him save them.

When you come up against a conflict or challenge, keep these powerful verses in mind. They'll alleviate your fears about the situation and your worries about how to handle it.

Then put yourself and your battle in God's hands. Go where He tells you to go. Knowing He's with you, calmly take your stand and watch God work His wonders.

I don't know what You're going to do, Lord,
but I know my role. I'll go where You tell me,
calmly stand there, and watch You work.

COURAGE TO SAY THE RIGHT THING

Everyone enjoys giving good advice, and how wonderful it is to be able to say the right thing at the right time!
PROVERBS 15:23 TLB

Our loved ones come to us for advice. The right thing to say might not be what they want to hear. If we hold back on our advice, heartache may ensue. If we go full force with our recommendations, the relationship might suffer. The first step is to pray for guidance.

We can take a cue from the One who always said the right thing at the right time. Jesus answered questions posed to Him with wise, thought-provoking questions, such as in Mark 10:17 (NASB), when a man asked Him, "Good Teacher, what shall I do to inherit eternal life?" Jesus' first reply was, "Why do you call Me good?" Did Jesus first want to establish that the man knew of His deity?

When we determine the real need, then we can offer the right advice with the courage to say the right thing at the right time.

Heavenly Father, remind us to look to You before offering our advice.

CREATIVE ENDEAVOR

*Then you will seek Me, inquire for, and require
Me [as a vital necessity] and find Me when
you search for Me with all your heart.*

JEREMIAH 29:13 AMPC

When we get out of our own heads and into God's head, seeking Him with *all our heart*, we tap into the creativity of the Creator. Possibilities abound. Ideas become limitless. His answers are often surprising, things we never thought of. The stress melts away as solutions pour down.

There's no need to think this heart-avenue is blocked, not open to you, that you are ill-equipped. For God says in Jeremiah 24:7 (ESV): "I will give them a heart to know that I am the LORD, and they shall be my people and I will be their God, for they shall return to me with their whole heart."

So what are you waiting for? Allow prayer to be your creative and limitless endeavor. Go to God. Seek Him with your whole heart, and He will expand your world.

I come to You, Lord, with my whole heart.

YOUR GREATEST WEAPONS

Jehoshaphat stopped and said, "Listen to me, all you people of Judah and Jerusalem! Believe in the Lord your God, and you will be able to stand firm. Believe in his prophets, and you will succeed."
2 Chronicles 20:20 nlt

After God had given King Jehoshaphat his marching orders, he told his people to believe in God, stand firm, and they'd see success in the mighty battle against them. Then he appointed singers to march out *in front of his army* and sing songs of praise to God. "At the very moment they began to sing and give praise, the Lord caused the armies. . .to start fighting among themselves" (2 Chronicles 20:22 nlt). By the time the army of Judah got to the battleground, there was nothing left for them to do but gather up the spoils.

Your greatest weapons against fear and worry are prayer and praise. Pray for guidance, and then praise the God you love and believe in. You'll be able not only to stand strong but to find treasures galore.

Lord, thank You for fighting for me. Your faithful love endures forever! (See 2 Chronicles 20:21.)

COURAGE TO USE RESTRAINT

When there are many words, transgression is unavoidable, but he who restrains his lips is wise.
Proverbs 10:19 nasb

Jephthah's unrestrained vow cost him his beloved daughter. A better word choice would've produced a happier outcome as he came home from battle.

Many times we've feared the backlash of words spoken in zeal or anger. We can't pull them back in after they've been released. The consequences of our words can be far-reaching, affecting family and friends, and even strangers, for generations.

Jesus said to the Pharisees in Matthew 12:34 (nasb), "For the mouth speaks out of that which fills the heart." If fire dwells in the heart, then sparks will come out of the mouth. The urge to respond, rebuke, or retaliate is often stronger than our ability to hold the tongue. There is wisdom in a ten-second pause to take a deep breath. Fear of the repercussions of hasty words can give us the courage to use restraint.

Heavenly Father, since we shall give an accounting for every careless word we speak, let our words reflect calm hearts filled with the love of Christ.

MEDITATIVE REFLECTION

Let the words of my mouth and the meditation of my heart be acceptable in Your sight, O Lord, my [firm, impenetrable] Rock and my Redeemer.
PSALM 19:14 AMPC

Philosopher Denis Diderot said, "There are three principal means of acquiring knowledge. . .observation of nature, reflection, and experimentation. Observation collects facts; reflection combines them; and experimentation verifies the result of that combination."

The more knowledge you have of God, the more you find yourself trusting Him and the less you stress. It's easy enough to observe Him, to collect facts about Him. But do you reflect on those facts? Do you allow them to bring you deeper into His arms? Do you open up and give Him access to your heart, so that He can come in and sup with you, lead you, love you? Do you incorporate your observations and reflections into your life, bringing God even more into your "reality"?

Consider these things. Then use them to grow deeper into your Rock and Redeemer.

Lord, make my meditation such that I would learn to know and love You more.

Day 93
COME AS YOU ARE

Let everyone come who is thirsty [who is painfully
conscious of his need of those things by which the
soul is refreshed, supported, and strengthened];
and whoever [earnestly] desires to do it, let him
come. . .and drink the water of Life without cost.
REVELATION 22:17 AMPC

Have you worried you aren't good enough to come to God
and unload your cares and concerns? That you aren't worthy
enough to ask for and receive God's mercy, Jesus' love, and the
Holy Spirit's help?

In the hymn "Come Ye Sinners," lyricist Joseph Hart provides these words: "Come, ye weary, heavy-laden / Lost and
ruined by the fall / If you tarry 'til you're better / You will never
come at all."

God knows you aren't perfect. That's why He sent Jesus to
save you and left the Holy Spirit to help you. So don't tarry.
Go to God and set your burdens down. Take up His light, and
you'll find refreshment for your soul, strength for your spirit,
and love for your heart.

I'm coming to You just as I am, Lord.
Take my worries and give me Your peace.

FEAR OF OUTCOMES

*We can make our plans, but the final
outcome is in God's hands.*
PROVERBS 16:1 TLB

The most famous upset in American voting history was the 1948 presidential election. Every prediction indicated the incumbent, President Harry Truman, would lose to New York governor Thomas Dewey. The *Chicago Daily Tribune* editors were so sure of the outcome, they printed an errant headline in advance.

Satan used Judas in his attempt to thwart God's plan for our salvation. His scheme backfired on him, but benefited those of us who believe in Jesus' sacrifice on the cross to pay for our sin.

The apostle Paul planned to go to Bithynia to preach the Word, but the Spirit of Jesus sent him to Macedonia instead. The outcome saved Paul from possible harm and brought the Gospel to Europe.

When making plans, we might fear the outcome because of unforeseen consequences. Will they backfire on us, like the 1948 election headline or bring unexpected benefits, like Paul's journey to Macedonia? Give that fear to God. It's in His hands.

*Almighty God, we find courage knowing
we can trust You in all outcomes.*

THE SON IS STILL THERE

*Fix your thoughts on what is true, and honorable,
and right, and pure, and lovely, and admirable.
Think about things that are excellent and worthy of praise.*
PHILIPPIANS 4:8 NLT

The apostle Paul had experienced his share of sickness, hunger, imprisonment, persecution, and more. He knew how easy it was for Jesus' followers to get stressed out, hung up on all the hazards of their faith facing them. But he also knew the secret of getting out from under all the negative news. His own rule and his advice to readers was to think about the good things.

Pay attention to what's running through your head. Fix your thoughts on higher things. As Gloria Gaither said, "Even in the winter, in the midst of the storm, the sun is still there. Somewhere above the clouds, it still shines and warms and pulls at the life buried deep inside the brown branches and frozen earth."

*Help me, Lord, to remember to keep my
thoughts on good things, like You, to rise
above the stresses and into Your light.*

BEING A BLESSING

We can't allow ourselves to get tired of living the right way. Certainly, each of us will receive everlasting life at the proper time, if we don't give up. Whenever we have the opportunity, we have to do what is good for everyone.
GALATIANS 6:9–10 GW

If you allow yourself to be bogged down by worry, you won't have the energy to focus on anything but those things that concern and affect you. With your eyes on only yourself, you can no longer take advantage of—or even *see*—opportunities to help someone else. You stop being a blessing to others.

God wants you to not just love Him and yourself but your neighbors: the people lying by the road, wounded and bleeding physically, emotionally, spiritually, financially, and mentally.

Today, get out of yourself and into God and others by doing something good for your neighbor, friend, relative, or a stranger. As soon as you start focusing on others, your worries will fade in the light of love.

I want to expand my vision, Lord, to help those in need. Show me who I can help and love in Your name.

FEAR OF BEING FALSELY ACCUSED

Do what is right; then if men speak against you, calling you evil names, they will become ashamed of themselves for falsely accusing you when you have only done what is good.

1 PETER 3:16 TLB

Joseph didn't complain as he endured prison after a false accusation. The Lord had already planned to put him in charge under Pharaoh in order to preserve the Israelites. Joseph fulfilled God's objective.

Paul and Silas, accused of inciting a riot, were beaten and jailed. An earthquake proved their faithfulness, bringing the jailer and his family to faith in the risen Christ. They fulfilled God's objective.

A false accusation could be as simple as a mistaken identity or as serious as a heinous crime. Would we have the courage to seek the Lord's plan in the harsh experience? He has a great purpose for each of us. Like Joseph, Paul, and Silas, let us fulfill God's objective.

Almighty God, when others hurl false accusations at us, give us courage to endure it as we await the fulfillment of Your objective.

LESSONS TO LEARN

"As it is written in the Scriptures, 'They will all be taught by God.' Everyone who listens to the Father and learns from him comes to me."

JOHN 6:45 NLT

Ralph Waldo Emerson said, "No man ever prayed heartily without learning something."

What is your prayer life like? Do you take the things that are stressing you out and present them to God? Do you put your entire heart into the endeavor? Do you ask God to show you what He wants you to see before you open up His Word? Are you persistently asking, seeking, and knocking on His door (see Matthew 7:7)? Are you allowing yourself to be vulnerable, letting Him into your world—heart, mind, body, spirit, and soul—opening the door where He is seeking entry (see Revelation 3:20)?

God has good things in store for you, wisdom to impart, words to heal, love to give, lessons to learn. Look. Listen. Learn.

Lord, I come before You, seeking You with my entire being. Teach me what You would have me know.

GOD MAKES YOUR PATHS PLAIN

*Trust in the LORD with all your heart, and do not
lean on your own understanding. In all your ways
acknowledge him, and he will make straight your paths.*
PROVERBS 3:5–6 ESV

At some point in your life, chances are you asked God to tell
you what He would have you do to serve Him, whether as a
missionary, pastor, wife, mother, writer, secretary, company
executive, mayor, and so on. And He answered your prayer,
directing you into an area that you already had a passion for.
But then, as the years passed, your passion ebbed a bit, and
now you're wondering if there is some new road He wants you
to take. Or you're worrying that maybe you had it wrong from
the very beginning!

Perhaps it's time to ask God again to show you which way
to go. Then trust Him to do so—but don't make a move until
He's made everything plain. Patience will be your reward.

*I'm leaning into and on You, Lord. Show me the
road You want me on. I'm trusting in You.*

FEAR OF MIRACLES

Then fear came upon every soul, and many wonders
and signs were done through the apostles.
ACTS 2:43 NKJV

A miracle is an extraordinary event that signifies God's presence in our human existence.

The Lord gave His apostles authority to perform signs and wonders. These miracles helped the early church grow under Peter's leadership.

Although miracles have occurred throughout history, many people still deny or fear them. They don't believe a miracle occurred, but merely a coincidence. Others argue the authority to perform miracles didn't extend beyond the apostles. Some fear seeking a miracle would take their eyes off the Lord.

Did a coincidence save survivors of an airplane crash? Where did the man who prayed over a child hit by a car get his authority to do so? Did the healing of a terminal illness sidetrack the former patient's focus on God?

Whether we witness a worldwide phenomenon or the everyday miracle of a blooming sunflower, let us utilize God's signs and wonders to lead others to Him.

Almighty God, thank You for miracles.
We praise You for the wondrous
signs that point us to You.

TIME-OUT

The Sovereign LORD. . .says: "Only in returning to me
and resting in me will you be saved. In quietness and
confidence is your strength." . . . Your own ears will hear
him. Right behind you a voice will say, "This is the way
you should go," whether to the right or to the left.
ISAIAH 30:15, 21 NLT

When a child gets a time-out from her parents, she may find
herself in a chair by herself, perhaps facing a wall. It's quiet with
no distractions at hand. No toys, books, TV, or radio allowed.
The period of sequestering is usually one minute for each year
of age, during which time the child has time to reflect and rest.
At the end, she's ready to go again—hopefully the right way.

When was the last time you took time out with God, returned to Him, rested in Him, and came away quieter within
and, having heard Him speak, more confident in Him? Try a
time-out with God today. The length is up to you—and Him.

Lord, I'm returning for rest in You today.

SUPERHUMAN POWER

When you received the message of God. . .you welcomed it
not as the word of [mere] men, but as it truly is, the Word
of God, which is effectually at work in you who believe
[exercising its superhuman power in those who
adhere to and trust in and rely on it].

1 Thessalonians 2:13 ampc

Imagine it! God's Word is working in you, "exercising its *superhuman* power" within you as you live it out, trusting in and relying on it!

God's Word is everything you need! It saves, guides, warns, rewards, and counsels you. It trains you up into the woman God has created you to be. It revives your spirit, restores your strength, comforts your heart, nourishes your soul, and renews your mind. It strengthens you, gives you joy, and prospers you.

Forget about the worries. Focus on the Word. And God will change you from the inside out!

I want to tap into Your superhuman power,
Lord. Take my worries into Your hands
and pour out Your Word upon me!

COURAGE NOT TO COMPROMISE

If a godly man compromises with the wicked, it is like polluting a fountain or muddying a spring.
PROVERBS 25:26 TLB

A compromise is a promise with concessions. We promise to give up ground on a transaction in exchange for a favorable position. Negotiation in real estate is a common practice and usually works well for both parties. However, yielding ground in defense of our faith obscures the clear Gospel of Jesus Christ.

Acquaintances offered their assistance during a difficult time, but they overshot the boundaries of helpfulness. God gave me the courage to submit a gracious, yet firm response. Although they meant well, I would not compromise my principles.

Abraham had the courage to not compromise when he took Isaac, his son—his only son—to offer as a sacrifice to the Lord. God honored Abraham's unfailing obedience and provided a substitution.

God will honor our faithfulness to Him, as He did Abraham, when we trust Him for the conclusion. Let Him provide the uncompromised alternative.

Gracious God, grant us the courage to not pollute the fountain of faith with which You have cleansed our hearts.

AN ENSOULED BEING

So those who received his word were baptized, and there
were added that day about three thousand souls.
And they devoted themselves to the apostles' teaching
and the fellowship, to the breaking of bread and the
prayers. And awe came upon every soul.
ACTS 2:41–43 ESV

C. S. Lewis said, "We don't have a soul. We are a soul. We happen to have a body."

How would your life change if you looked at it from the perspective of your being a soul that just happens to be inhabiting a body? According to HELPS Word-studies, the word *soul* used in the verses above corresponds to the Old Testament word for "soul": "The *soul* is the direct aftermath of God breathing (blowing) His gift of life into a person, making them an *ensouled being*" (emphasis added).

See yourself as an eternal creature who has been given God's breath of life, who has been endowed with a soul, and you'll find yourself more awed than anxious.

I am Your breath within a body, Lord.
Help me live Your way.

MEDITATE ON WONDERS

*Every day [with its new reasons] will I bless You
[affectionately and gratefully praise You]; yes,
I will praise Your name forever and ever. . . .
On the glorious splendor of Your majesty and
on Your wondrous works I will meditate.*

PSALM 145:2, 5 AMPC

David, the shepherd boy who turned king, loved to talk to God. Many of his psalms speak of his fears, woes, and worries. But David also looked for the good in his life. He actively kept his eyes open for the new and amazing things the Lord was doing every day and praised God for them. Then he would keep God's wonders in mind all day long.

Why not follow David's example? After unloading your worries, actively seek something new to praise God for. Keep your eyes open to His wonders and works around you. Think about them throughout your day. You'll find yourself so busy looking for the good, you won't have time to worry.

*Today I'm looking for new reasons to praise
and adore You, Lord! On Your works
and wonders I will meditate!*

COURAGE TO STAY THE COURSE

And the Lord shall deliver me from every evil work,
and will preserve me unto his heavenly kingdom:
to whom be glory for ever and ever. Amen.
2 TIMOTHY 4:18 KJV

Understanding the time we live in makes determining what to do more confusing. In Paul's charge to Timothy—and to us—we are supposed to preach the Word of God in an instant. Not only with our words, but with our actions too.

We can reprove, rebuke, and exhort even when those we'll share the Gospel with don't want to follow sound doctrine. They would rather listen to ear-tickling stories than hear that Jesus died for their sins.

Paul started his good fight on the road to Damascus and ended with his death. Our good fight began the moment we accepted Christ as our Savior. With Him at our side, we will be watchful, patient, and bear unknown afflictions as we stay the course for the sake of the Gospel.

Glorious Father, stand with us and strengthen us so
that we can be Your vessels to deliver Your truth.

ALWAYS AND ALL WAYS

*God is our refuge and strength, a very present help
in trouble. Therefore we will not fear though the
earth gives way, though the mountains be
moved into the heart of the sea.*

PSALM 46:1–2 ESV

The author of Psalm 46 would have you remember a very calming fact: God is there for you, right beside you, a fortress to which you can run and hide, your very strength in times of trouble—no matter what that trouble is, where it is happening, or to whom it is happening. Because of that fact, there really is no reason to stress or strain. As the psalmist goes on to explain, there is absolutely nothing that God cannot handle, no tide He cannot turn, no fire He cannot quench, no lion He cannot tame. Remember this truth.

God says, "Be still, and know that I am God" (Psalm 46:10 ESV). *You* are not. But *He* is. And He is with you—always and in all ways.

*Thank You, Lord, for being the one and
only true God. Help me be still in You.*

Day 108

THAT SPECIAL GLOW

*"If you are generous with the hungry and start
giving yourselves to the down-and-out, your lives
will begin to glow in the darkness, your shadowed
lives will be bathed in sunlight."*

ISAIAH 58:10 MSG

When your worries become a shadow in your life, get out of yourself and into others. Find a food pantry you can donate to. Consider volunteering at the next Thanksgiving meal at a local soup kitchen. Weed a widow's garden, offer to drive a carless person to church, or help support a child who lives in poverty.

As you expend your energy to help others, you will begin to glow in this dark world. Your shadowed life will be bathed in God's Son's light. And you'll find people saying, "I want what she has." There's no better witness than that.

*Lord, I want to get out from underneath this shadow
of worry. Open my eyes to the needs around me.
What can I do today to help someone, become a
powerful force in Your kingdom, and brighten
up my own life—all at the same time?*

COURAGE TO BREAK MAN'S LAW TO OBEY GOD

"Let it be known to you, O king, that we are not going to serve your gods or worship the golden image that you have set up."

DANIEL 3:18 NASB

Shadrach, Meshach, and Abednego believed that God would deliver them from Nebuchadnezzar's hand, even if deliverance meant death in the fiery furnace.

It is illegal to openly worship Jesus in some countries. Even courts in the United States have drawn a faint line in the sand, obscuring the language of our Constitution. Our freedom of speech is violated when we are denied the right to pray in Christ's name or share our love for Him in public. Jesus warned that we would be hated because of His name. Litigious unbelievers bring lawsuits against us, and courts subject us to heavy fines for adhering to our Christian faith.

Our reward for trusting in God will surpass any penalty the courts may impose on us.

Father God, give us the courage to break man's law when it's necessary to obey Your laws. Let us rejoice and be glad, for our rewards in heaven are great.

INCLINED TO PRAY

"Incline your ear, O LORD, and hear;
open your eyes, O LORD, and see."
2 KINGS 19:16 ESV

Talk about being stressed. King Hezekiah and his kingdom of Judah were being threatened at the gates, and his God was being bad-mouthed by the very powerful king of Assyria who then put his threats and insults in a letter to Hezekiah.

But Hezekiah didn't freak out. He went to God and spread the letter before Him. Then he prayed, praising God for all His power. Asking Him to hear and see what was happening in his life. Asking God to save him—so that everyone would see that He alone was God.

The result? "That night the angel of the LORD went out and struck down 185,000 in the camp of the Assyrians. . . . Then Sennacherib king of Assyria departed" (2 Kings 19:35–36 ESV).

If God could do this for Hezekiah, imagine what He can do for you!

Lord, I know You are amazing. Hear and see me.
Help me, so that all will know You alone are God!

NEW HOPE EVERY MORNING

*There's one other thing I remember, and
remembering, I keep a grip on hope: God's
loyal love couldn't have run out, his merciful
love couldn't have dried up. They're created new
every morning. How great your faithfulness!*
LAMENTATIONS 3:21–22 MSG

You may find that some wounds seem harder to heal than others
or that some worries keep cropping up.

Take heart. Keep your grip on hope by remembering that
God's love and mercy never run out or dry up. Every morning
your Creator has a new supply that you can access through
spending time in His Word, praying, and meditating. Just give
God room and time to speak through the Spirit. Open yourself
to some new thoughts. God, in His faithfulness, will meet you
just where you need Him the most.

*Lord, in times of doubt, trial, and worry, remind
me that You are always there for me with a new
supply of love and mercy every morning. Speak
deep into my heart. And I will praise Your
never-ending faithfulness to me!*

FEAR OF INJUSTICE

"Be very much afraid to give any other decision than
what God tells you. For there must be no injustice
among God's judges, no partiality, no taking of bribes."
2 CHRONICLES 19:7 TLB

Judges aren't allowed to counsel with Almighty God, although they should. Moved by compassion for a repeat criminal begging for another chance, a judge could impose a lighter sentence. That same judge might throw the book at a first-time offender, ignorant of judicial procedures.

At times, they render unmerited verdicts because of their own biases. The guilty go free, and the innocent are jailed, depending on the attorneys' legal knowledge and persuasiveness with the court.

The duty of Supreme Court justices calls for them to base their opinions on the facts presented. But they can bring their own preconceived attitudes to the bench. It's possible they'll follow the prevailing wind, especially in high-profile, media-blitzed cases.

Like us, they're flawed human beings in need of the Lord.

Dear God, help us to replace our fear
of injustice with prayers for our judges,
elected and appointed. Give them courage
to consult You for their decisions.

Day 113

CLOSE TO HIS HEART

He will feed his flock like a shepherd.
He will carry the lambs in his arms,
holding them close to his heart.
ISAIAH 40:11 NLT

You are in the Great Shepherd's arms. You have no need to fear. To struggle. To panic. You are in the safest place you could ever be. In the arms of the One who loves you beyond compare, who sacrificed His life so that you could be with Him forever. He is watching over you. He's the barrier between you and that which could harm you. He is the One who meets all your needs. He leads you down the right paths, to clean, living water and food that satisfies.

So be still. Relax in His arms. Lean back. Breathe deep. Feel His heartbeat. You are home. Let Him carry you.

Lord, here I am, leaning back against You,
listening to Your heartbeat, feeling Your breath
and the warmth of Your love. Hold me tight.
Keep me close forevermore.

SWEET-SMELLING INCENSE

Is anyone crying for help?
GOD is listening, ready to rescue you.
PSALM 34:17 MSG

Do you sometimes wonder if God is listening to you? Do you worry your prayers are falling on deaf ears?

Don't. It's the evil one who wants you to think God neither hears nor cares about your worries, problems, and questions. It's the father of lies' aim to drive a wedge between you and the Lord. Yet the truth is that every word you utter in prayer rises up to God like sweet-smelling incense (see Revelation 8:4).

As you go to God in prayer today, imagine Him eagerly waiting to hear what you have to say. See Him hanging on every word. Then take the time to listen to His response. His words will rescue you, bringing you ever closer to Him.

GOD, come close. Come quickly! Open your ears—it's my voice you're hearing! Treat my prayer as sweet incense rising; my raised hands are my evening prayers (Psalm 141:1–2 MSG).

FEAR OF BEING CAUGHT DOING WRONG

Nathan then said to David, "You are the man!"
2 SAMUEL 12:7 NASB

When King David's efforts to conceal his treachery failed, he compounded his sin of adultery with murder.

Nathan's story of a poor man's ewe lamb opened David's eyes to the extent of his crimes.

David received the rebuke with a contrite heart, and confessed his sin against the Lord. His selfish acts slandered God's good name.

Although God forgave David, the far-reaching consequences of his sin remained. The child conceived in adultery would die, and David's kingdom would come to ruin. Severe offenses call for serious punishment.

How often have we tried to hide evidence of our wrongs? Do we need a Nathan to give us a glimpse into our own hearts?

God is omniscient. He sees directly into our hearts. Repentance means agreeing with the Lord about our sin. While we are forgiven through Christ, the consequences of our actions must be addressed.

Father in heaven, whether caught or not, please give us the courage to confess our sins and the strength to assume the consequences.

EVERYTHING WILL BE FINE

The LORD replied, "I will personally go with you. . .
and I will give you rest—everything will be fine for you."
EXODUS 33:14 NLT

Whenever she heard concern in an adult's voice or saw a furrowed brow, three-year-old Emmaleen would respond with, "It'll be *fine*." Over and over again, she blessed the lives and calmed the qualms of many with her little mantra, "It'll be *fine*." How did she arrive at this conclusion? How did it become such a big part of her own life and personality as the years went by? These three little words were the same ones Emmaleen's mother often imparted to her.

God wants you to get the same message, repeat the same mantra, know the same truth. That no matter what has happened, is happening, or might happen, God is with you. He is personally at your side. He will give you rest. "Everything will be fine for you."

Help me to have the faith and trust of a three-year-old, Lord. Help me to see that with You right next to me, it'll be fine.

THE REALITY OF FAITH

Now faith is the assurance (the confirmation, the title deed) of the things [we] hope for, being the proof of things [we] do not see and the conviction of their reality [faith perceiving as real fact what is not revealed to the senses].

HEBREWS 11:1 AMPC

Worry is often prompted by fear, which some people say stands for False Evidence Appearing Real. Yet God would have you overcome those worries and fears with faith in Him and His Word. Faith is not wishful thinking but *knowing* God has made certain promises to you and that He will keep those promises. So you can accept them as your present reality even if you do not yet perceive them.

As you read the Bible, you begin to see and understand that all God has said and promised came to pass for those who believed. And this same fact holds true for you today. So let go of fears and worries, and hang on to faith and hope. God is already working on your behalf, transforming His promises into your reality even as you read these words.

I believe, Lord. I believe.

COURAGE TO ADMIT WE'RE WRONG

*Then Nathan said to David, . . . "Why did you
despise the word of the LORD by doing what is evil
in his eyes?". . . Then David said to Nathan,
"I have sinned against the LORD."*
2 SAMUEL 12:7, 9, 13 NIV

The Lord sent Nathan to confront David about his sin. The prophet
Nathan gave David an introspective scrutiny into his own heart
with the story of the poor man's ewe lamb (see 2 Samuel 12:1–5).

David's crimes, though committed in secret, had to be
judged publicly. God said he had "given great occasion to the
enemies of the LORD to blaspheme" (verse 14 KJV). He confessed
his transgression against the Lord.

God forgave him, but the far-reaching consequences of his
actions remained. The child conceived in sin would die, and
David's future kingdom would come to ruin.

Admitting our guilt takes courage, especially when faced
with the repercussions. It's tempting to pervert God's Word to
justify our behavior or blame someone else. Our immediate
confession will always be met with God's grace. The consequences of our bad behavior, however, cannot be averted. We've
damaged God's name.

*Gracious Father, Your forgiveness will
bring comfort, and Your mercy will
grant us courage as we endure the
plight set in motion by our sin.*

YOUR VERY BREATH

They should seek God, in the hope that they might feel after Him and find Him, although He is not far from each one of us. For in Him we live and move and have our being.

ACTS 17:27–28 AMPC

God is not some distant, foreign deity. He is closer than your very breath. St. Gregory of Nazianzus advised us, "Remember God more often than you breathe."

Imagine thinking of God with each inhale and exhale. Pause in this moment and feel that breath. Feel God's presence. Recognize He is above, below, within, and without. With these ideas at the forefront of your mind and the awareness of His love in the depths of your soul, there is no room for fight, flight, or freeze. Only peace as you live, move, and have your being.

Lord, You are not some piece of wood or stone.
You are a living God who is working in my life,
taking care of me, and bringing me peace
and contentment in this very moment
as I live and breathe.

WORDS OF LIFE

Remember what you said to me, your servant—
I hang on to these words for dear life!
These words hold me up in bad times;
yes, your promises rejuvenate me.
P SALM 119:49–50 MSG

When you're going through a hard time, burdened by worries, there is only one place where you can find comfort: God's Word. It is there alone that you'll find your strength, nourishment, comfort, and hope.

If you're so troubled and worried that you can't even think, the best Bible book to go to is the Psalms. It's like reading someone's personal journal. The psalmists write of their troubles, fears, doubts, worries, and hardships. Yet they find reasons to praise God for all the wonderful things He is doing and has done in the past and they are certain He will do in the future.

Hang on to God's words. They will speak to your heart, lift your spirit, and soothe your soul.

Dear God, I long for Your comfort. Show me in Your Word what You would have me read, know, and study. Hold me up with Your precious words!

FEAR OF GUILT

And their sins and iniquities will I remember no more.
HEBREWS 10:17 KJV

We've accepted Christ's gift of redemption for our sins. All our wicked acts—past, present, and future—are buried at the foot of Jesus' cross. Yet guilt creeps back into our minds, bringing with it the darkness of remorse. We linger on them, like a cow chewing her cud, trying to grind away the shame.

Those dreadful thoughts are not from the Holy Spirit, but from the adversary. Satan's accusing finger constantly pokes at us, jabbing us right in the heart, prodding us to doubt and fear.

God has forgiven our sins and remembers them no more. What logical reason do we have to focus on them?

When the devil attempts to strike fear in us with memories of our dastardly deeds, our best defense is to turn them into praises to God.

Merciful Father, You have cleansed us of the terrible acts we have done, continue to do, and will do in the future. Thank You for Your loving mercy and willingness to forgive and forget our guiltiness.

BREAKING CHAINS

Paul and Silas were praying and singing hymns to
God. . . . Suddenly, there was a massive earthquake,
and the prison was shaken to its foundations.
All the doors immediately flew open, and
the chains of every prisoner fell off!
ACTS 16:25–26 NLT

"Prayer is not only worship; it is also an invisible emanation of man's worshiping spirit—the most powerful form of energy that one can generate," wrote Nobel Prize winner Alexis Carrel, MD.

Prayer is a force that can shake open doors, make chains fall away, and set prisoners free. With all this power, prayer obviously can release your stress, make your burdens fall away, and change your limited perspective. All you need to do is believe it is possible. When you do, you will be singing with the chorus, "Our Lord is great, with limitless strength" (Psalm 147:5 MSG).

I want to tap into Your power, Lord.
I know nothing is too hard or impossible for You.
Help me to have a strong prayer life that breaks chains.

FELLOW WORRIERS

*Peace I leave with you; My [own] peace I now give and
bequeath to you. Not as the world gives do I give to you.
Do not let your hearts be troubled, neither let
them be afraid. [Stop allowing yourselves to be
agitated and disturbed. . .and unsettled.]*
JOHN 14:27 AMPC

Lately you've found yourself in a pretty good place, each day
dutifully handing your worries over to God and tapping into
Jesus' peace through prayer. But then someone comes along
venting his or her own worries. Before you know it, the worries
you thought you'd left behind are rearing up all over again.
What's a woman to do?

Be a good listener, but don't let someone else's fears trigger
your own. Simply pray for your fellow worrier with the real-
ization that his or her worries are what they see as truth. But
you know better. For *your* truth lies in the Word of life. You
have Jesus to give you the peace you need and the wisdom to
know that, in God, all is truly well.

With You, Jesus, I'm a fellow warrior not a worrier!

COURAGE TO BE FREE

For you were called to freedom, brethren; only do not
turn your freedom into an opportunity for the flesh,
but through love serve one another.
GALATIANS 5:13 NASB

Freedom isn't free.

World history proves that too much freedom can be fatal. It leads to apathy, which leads to anarchy, which leads to slavery, which leads to destruction of our liberty.

God created us with a basic need to be free. Adam enjoyed freedom until he rebelled against his Creator. His apathy toward Eve made her vulnerable to the serpent. Adam and Eve became anarchists when Eve blamed the serpent, and Adam blamed God. Their choices enslaved them to Satan.

Jesus set us free from the slavery of sin. We must remain diligent not to slip back into the shackles of our base desires, diminishing the significance of Christ's ultimate sacrifice. Our earthly lusts are fed by selfishness. Offering our service in Christian love keeps our focus off ourselves and on the Lord.

> *O God our Creator, we praise You for giving*
> *us the courage to keep the freedom that*
> *Christ's death on the cross provided.*

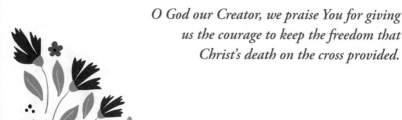

STEER CLEAR

He drew me up out of a horrible pit [a pit of tumult and of destruction], out of the miry clay (froth and slime), and set my feet upon a rock, steadying my steps and establishing my goings.
PSALM 40:2 AMPC

God has a threefold process to get you up out of the pit of needless stress. First, He'll pull you to *safety*. Then He'll set your feet on solid ground and help you find your balance again, giving you *security*. Finally, He'll guide you to the next venture, helping you *steer clear* of future pitfalls. Afterward, you'll be singing a new tune, praising God. Others will notice what's happening in your life and find themselves wanting what you have and trusting more in the Lord.

The only thing you need to do is reach out to Him. Let Him know what's going on in your life. He will listen. He will see. He will reach down and lift you up to safety, give you the security you crave, and help you steer clear of snags.

I'm so ready, Lord. Pull me up to You!

GOOD SPIRITUALITY

Be happy [in your faith] and rejoice and be glad-
hearted continually (always); be unceasing in prayer
[praying perseveringly]; thank [God] in everything [no
matter what the circumstances may be, be thankful and
give thanks], for this is the will of God for you.
1 Thessalonians 5:16–18 ampc

Inventor William Painter said, "Saying thank you is more than good manners. It is good spirituality." The apostle Paul, author of Thessalonians, is in complete agreement.

Instead of worrying, God wants you to rejoice continually, to pray without ceasing, and to thank God for everything—"no matter what the circumstances may be." That may sound like a really tall order, but if that's what God wants and wills you to do, He'll give you the power and strength to do it! Besides, if you begin to spend all your time rejoicing, praying, and thanking God, you won't have time to worry!

Help me, Lord, to seek constant joy in You.
To pray continually, giving You my worries
as soon as they creep into my mind then
leaving them in Your hands. I thank You
no matter what happens or when!

COURAGE TO VOTE

"Moreover you shall select from all the people able men,
such as fear God, men of truth, hating covetousness;
and place such over them to be rulers of thousands,
rulers of hundreds, rulers of fifties, and rulers of tens."
EXODUS 18:21 NKJV

Hidden in God's instructions to Moses for selecting righteous leaders is an organizational pyramid.

This shape reflects our elective process. The base, or bottom of the pyramid, signifies our national offices—rulers of thousands.

Above that is our regional level—rulers of hundreds.

Next up is our state level—rulers of fifties.

The apex, our local offices, is the most important level—rulers of tens. Local elections are far more effective because, at this stage, we control who reaches the descending levels. We can defeat or promote a candidate at the city or county elections, even by one vote.

Considering our local elections as a top-down process might give us the needed courage to exercise our moral obligation and vote—every time.

Father God, we pray for courage to select men and
women who are eager to serve according to Your will.

HOLDING NOTHING BACK

*GOD met me more than halfway, he freed me from my
anxious fears. Look at him; give him your warmest smile.
Never hide your feelings from him. When I was desperate,
I called out, and GOD got me out of a tight spot.*

PSALM 34:4–6 MSG

Hannah is a great example of how to approach God in prayer.
While under great stress, and having already cried a river of
tears, Hannah went to the temple. She "was in distress of soul,
praying to the Lord and weeping bitterly" (1 Samuel 1:10 AMPC).
She told God everything! She made promises and continued
praying before Him silently—"speaking in her heart; only her
lips moved but her voice was not heard" (1 Samuel 1:13 AMPC).

God hears your prayers, whether said aloud or silently. And
when you look to Him for help, bearing your heart to Him,
He will meet you more than halfway. He'll free you from stress
and fear. He'll rescue you. What are you waiting for?

*Lord, I pour out my heart to You right now,
holding nothing back. Free me!*

REGAINING A FOOTHOLD OF FAITH

When I said, "My feet are slipping," your mercy,
O LORD, continued to hold me up. When I worried about
many things, your assuring words soothed my soul.
PSALM 94:18–19 GW

When you start to slip into worrying, when your feet of faith start to lose their purchase, tell God all about it. Acknowledge to yourself that His kindness and compassion *will help* you regain a foothold. Allow His words to soothe your soul and nurture your spirit.

No matter when worry, trouble, or danger strikes, God is right there with you in the midst of things. He promises He'll never leave your side.

Norman Vincent Peale wrote, "Frequently remind yourself that God is with you, that He will never fail you, that you can count upon Him. Say these words, 'God is with me, helping me.'" As you say these words, envision God right next to you, and your faith will prevail.

Lord, thank You for always being there when I need
You, loving me, holding me up, helping me out,
and soothing my soul.

FEAR OF GOVERNMENT

"You shall surely set a king over you
whom the LORD your God chooses."
DEUTERONOMY 17:15 NASB

Thomas Jefferson wisely said, "When the people fear the government, there is tyranny. When the government fears the people, there is liberty." He understood that a critical role of our government was to listen to the people.

At the adjournment of the Constitutional Convention in 1787, a woman asked Benjamin Franklin, "Well, Doctor, what have we got, a republic or a monarchy?"

Mr. Franklin answered, "A republic, if you can keep it."

Those prudent delegates used Deuteronomy 17:14–20 as guidance for creating our Constitution, emphasizing God-ordained restrictions on elected leaders.

Our three-pronged republic is comparable to a three-legged stool. If one leg grows too long, the stool topples. Fearful tyranny creeps in.

More than two hundred years later, ignorance and corruption have dimmed the foundations of that biblical example. God's Word teaches that the only incorruptible government will be during the thousand-year reign of Christ. Until He returns, we look to God for courage.

Come quickly, Lord!

Gracious Father, You guided our founding
fathers. Please direct our leaders back to You.

CIRCLE OF PROTECTION

*GOD's angel sets up a circle of protection around us
while we pray. Open your mouth and taste, open your
eyes and see—how good GOD is. Blessed are you who
run to him. Worship GOD if you want the best;
worship opens doors to all his goodness.*
PSALM 34:7–9 MSG

Amid a stressful situation in which you see no way out—
mentally, physically, emotionally, spiritually—go to God. As
soon as you're in His presence, He'll set up, between you and
whatever's coming against you, a protective barrier. See it. Know
it's there. Do not doubt. Then open your mouth and pray.
Realize how good God is. Praise Him for what He's doing in
your life. Know that even if you still don't see a way out, that's
okay. You're with the Master Planner and Protector. He's got
you covered. He has an exit plan. He has good things lined up
and coming your way. Then rest in His peace.

*I see no way out of this, Lord, but I know You do.
And in You I trust. In You I have peace.*

REFUGE, SHIELD, HOPE, AND PEACE

*You are my refuge and my shield; your word is my
source of hope. . . . Those who love your instructions
have great peace and do not stumble.*
PSALM 119:114, 165 NLT

When you're worried, lost, and confused, when you don't know where to go or who to turn to, go to God and open His Word. There you will find the refuge you so desperately seek, the safety you need, the hope you thirst for, and the compass you crave.

You can run to God no matter where you are for He is as near to you as your breath. Within His presence and power, you will be shielded. There you can wait until you have gained His wisdom and peace, until you know what to say or do. God will speak into your heart. He will make sure you do not stumble as you follow His instructions and take the next steps.

*Thank You, Lord, for being my constant refuge,
shield, and hope. In Your Word alone do
I find wisdom and peace.*

COURAGE IN DEFEAT

*And it came to pass, when Moses held up his
hand, that Israel prevailed: and when he let
down his hand, Amalek prevailed.*

EXODUS 17:11 KJV

Where there is victory, there is also a defeat. It is an outcome for every challenge, whether in battle, a sporting event, or the workplace.

So many struggles we face weigh us down. Using our own strength, we grow weaker and weaker until defeat overcomes us.

In the battle against Amalek, Moses grew weary from holding up the staff of God. Aaron and Hur provided a stone for him to sit. They stood on either side of him, bolstering up his arms.

God could have held up the staff, relieving Moses of the responsibility of Israel's fate. But He wanted to show us the importance of solidarity. Moses needed the help of his brother and brother-in-law.

As a team, we pull together and strengthen each other, even in the midst of defeat. Unaided, we face it alone.

*Almighty God, give us the strength to support
others facing trials, and the courage to ask
for help in our own struggles.*

CATCH YOUR BREATH

Is anyone crying for help? GOD is listening, ready to rescue you. If your heart is broken, you'll find GOD right there; if you're kicked in the gut, he'll help you catch your breath. Disciples so often get into trouble; still, GOD is there every time.

PSALM 34:17–19 MSG

The word *stress* has an interesting etymology, coming in part from words meaning "narrowness," "oppression," and "drawn tight." So it makes sense that when you're under stress you may feel as if the walls are closing in on you. As if your chest is drawn tight. It's almost hard to breathe.

On the one hand, there is stress, a sense of suffocation. On the other hand, there is God. The key is to remember God in the midst of your stress. To remember He is listening and ready to rescue you, to help you catch your breath. He'll do it every time. His job is to be there for you. Your job is to reach out for Him.

Help me catch my breath, Lord!

GOD'S ARM

Be the arm [of Your servants—their strength and defense]
every morning, our salvation in the time of trouble.
ISAIAH 33:2 AMPC

Author E. M. Bounds wrote, "If God is not first in our thoughts and efforts in the morning, he will be in the last place the remainder of the day." The Bible says King David sought God's guidance through early morning prayer (see Psalm 143:8). Even Jesus, long before the sun rose, went out alone to a deserted place and prayed to God (see Mark 1:35).

It's obvious that starting your day with prayer, seeking to make God your primary guide and focus instead of your own self, sets you on the right course. Before you're out the door, you'll be armed with God's strength, protection, and saving power. The volume of His voice in your heart, mind, and soul will then rise above all other sounds and whistles, keeping your feet on the right path and worries and other distractors at bay (see Isaiah 33:3).

Lord, be my strength and defense every morning.

COURAGE NOT TO ENVY OTHERS

Do not let your heart envy sinners,
but live in the fear of the Lord always.
Proverbs 23:17 nasb

Envy is a green-eyed monster. It creeps in as admiration for something someone else has. Then, if we allow, that admiration grows until we desire to have the item for ourselves. It's out of our reach. Not affordable or practical, but we still desire it. Then the green-eyed monster develops into full-blown covetousness. That's when we want someone else's property so much, that we'll take it by force. Nothing good comes from envy.

We might not know how the other person acquired the item we desire. Was it by theft or coercion from their own covetousness? Or was it a gift from the Lord for righteous living?

The sin of envy spits in God's eye. It says to Him, "You haven't given me enough. I want what others have."

In prayer, we can turn away the green-eyed monster before it lures us away from trusting God.

Lord, let us be content in what You have provided.
We know You want only the best for Your children.

BOLD SOUL

I give you thanks, O LORD, with my whole heart. . . .
On the day I called, you answered me;
my strength of soul you increased.
PSALM 138:1, 3 ESV

Consider the fact that on the day you call on God, He answers you. Open yourself up to the idea that as soon as you cry out, He responds, just as a breastfeeding mother automatically—physically, mentally, emotionally—responds to the cry of her newborn, ready to succor her little one at the first sign of hunger.

That's how God responds to you. He not only answers you but gives you so much strength in your soul that you are emboldened, able to overcome the fight, flight, and freeze reactions. He gives you the power to let go of worldly anxiety, replacing stress with His strength and boldness of spirit.

Call. He'll respond and give you all the strength you need. Then thank Him with your whole heart.

You amaze me, Lord, with how quickly You respond
to my cry. I thank You for giving me strength!

WARDING OFF WORRIES

*O Lord God, my savior, I cry out to you during the day
and at night. Let my prayer come into your presence.
Turn your ear to hear my cries.*
Psalm 88:1–2 GW

Cynthia Lewis says, "If your day is hemmed in with prayer, it
is less likely to come unraveled." Let's take that a step further
and say that if your day is hemmed in with prayer, *you're* less
likely to come unraveled!

Chances are you brush your teeth in the morning and again
in the evening. You were taught to do this as a child and now
do it automatically, without even thinking. And that's a good
thing, for brushing teeth helps ward off cavities.

So why not start the practice of praying in the morning
and then again in the evening. As you do this day after day, it
too will become something you do automatically. And it'll be a
good thing because doing so will help ward off worries, giving
you a focused mind by day and a restful one at night!

*Lord, let my prayer come into Your
loving presence day and night.*

FEAR OF WORLDLY INFLUENCE

Then Jesus said to him, "Away with you, Satan!
For it is written, 'You shall worship the LORD
your God, and Him only you shall serve.' "
MATTHEW 4:10 NKJV

How presumptive of Satan to offer Christ what He already owns. The world and all that is in it belongs to God.

In his shrewd methods to lure us away from the Lord, Satan lies about the consequences of following his dark path. He doesn't disclose that a life of partying brings death by alcoholism, drug addiction, and disease. Enticements of "wealth by stealth" bankrupt our trust in each other. He says it's okay to lie, cheat, and steal. Everyone does it.

Jesus countered each of Satan's temptations with the Word of God. He gave us a powerful weapon to keep us in step with Him.

As worldly influences rush at us like water from a fire hydrant, let us weigh them against the Bible. Through prayer and studying the scriptures, we can submit to God's influence instead of acquiescing to Satan's world.

Gracious Lord, thank You for Your Holy
Word to fortify us against the devil.

SAFE AND SOUND

No one stood by me. They all ran like scared rabbits.
But it doesn't matter—the Master stood by me
and helped me. . . . God's looking after me,
keeping me safe in the kingdom of heaven.
2 TIMOTHY 4:16–18 MSG

Are you aware of God's care all the time? Do you know that no matter what troubles you step in the middle of, He won't leave you alone? He has a long and loving reach. There is nothing He cannot turn around to work for your good. You may not see it now, but that's okay. You will someday. He has His hand on you. His love and protection are never ending.

So take heart. God is working out all plans in your favor. Just continue hoping, trusting, praying. Your deliverer is right next to you, standing by you, keeping you safe and sound!

Lord, one thing that keeps me going is knowing
I'm not alone. You are forever with me,
loving me, helping me, rescuing me.

THE PEACE OF GOD'S KINGDOM

Now may the Lord of peace Himself grant you His peace
(the peace of His kingdom) at all times and in all ways
[under all circumstances and conditions, whatever comes].

2 THESSALONIANS 3:16 AMPC

The philosopher Michel de Montaigne, who lived in the 1500s, said: "My life has been filled with terrible misfortune; most of which never happened." Chances are that if you looked closely at your own life, you'd agree.

And there are modern-day statistics to back up Montaigne's statement. A recent study says 40 percent of the things you worry about will never happen; 30 percent are in the past, which you can't change; 12 percent are needless worries about your health; and 10 percent are trivial worries that fall into the miscellaneous category. That leaves you with 8 percent of worries that have actual substance in your life.

So tell your worries to hit the road, and walk in God's path of peace.

Lord of peace, fill me with Your presence and
the peace of Your kingdom at all times
and in all ways, whatever comes.

COURAGE TO STAND, STRIVE, AND SUFFER

*But Joseph reported to his father some
of the bad things they were doing.*
GENESIS 37:2 TLB

"The sin of doing nothing is the deadliest of all sins," the Reverend Charles F. Aked said in his 1916 speech, in favor of prohibition.

Standing for a righteous issue, like Rev. Aked, takes courage. The deeper the controversy, the more proponents on both sides have at stake.

We'll strive against those who fear losing money or status, which might cost us our income or position.

We'll suffer more than indignation. Friendships and sometimes families are ripped apart. We might encounter property damage, slander, or personal threats.

Joseph had to stand, strive, and suffer. Giving Jacob a bad report about his brothers, he had to stand for his honesty. Striving against them, their plot to kill him landed him in an empty well. He suffered the loss of home and family as his brothers sold him to foreigners. Yet, he remained faithful to the Lord.

*Righteous God, embolden us as You did Joseph
in times when we are called to stand,
strive, and suffer for integrity.*

LOOKS *ARE* EVERYTHING

Seeing Peter and John about to go into the temple,
he asked to receive alms. And Peter directed his gaze
at him, as did John, and said, "Look at us."
And he fixed his attention on them, expecting
to receive something from them.
ACTS 3:3–5 ESV

How do you begin your day? With a sense of helplessness and hopelessness? Are you looking for signs that somehow you'll eke out something good? Or are you fixing your attention on Jesus, expecting that He'll give you something beyond the best?

The beggar outside the temple thought he knew what he needed and that money was what Peter and John would give him. When told to look at them, the beggar did so, "expecting to receive something." What he got was something much more valuable than silver or gold. He received the power of Jesus Christ working in his life.

Put no limits on God. Simply look to Jesus and expect beyond the best!

As I begin this day, Lord, I'm looking for You and
Your power to do something amazing in my life.
My eyes are fixed on You!

— Day 144 —

GIVE GOD A CALL

*For you, O Lord, are good and forgiving, abounding
in steadfast love to all who call upon you. Give ear,
O LORD, to my prayer; listen to my plea for grace. In the
day of my trouble I call upon you, for you answer me.*
PSALM 86:5–7 ESV

No one is perfect—except God, of course. But you're a mere human. You're bound to make a few mistakes. There will probably be times when you wrong yourself, God, or a fellow human being. Before you realize it, you're caught in a whirl of worry—about the effects of your misstep, what God and others may be thinking about you (and your words and actions), how or what you'll say when you ask for forgiveness, and so on.

To break free of this whirl of worry, call on God. Remind yourself how forgiving He is, how much He loves you. Ask Him to hear your prayer and to bestow His forgiveness, and then expect His answer.

> *Lord, I'm calling on You, counting on Your
> love and forgiveness. Hear my prayer.
> Tell me how to handle this situation.*

Day 145

COURAGE TO SUFFER FOR RIGHTEOUSNESS' SAKE

*But even if you should suffer for righteousness'
sake, you are blessed. "And do not be afraid
of their threats, nor be troubled."*

1 PETER 3:14 NKJV

We are targets for censorship if we dare to pray in Jesus' name in a public place. Unbelievers file lawsuits against us if we object to being forced to accept the world's immorality. Courts penalize us with steep fines for holding to our Christian convictions. These are frightening times, yes, but we aren't tied to posts in an arena filled with hungry lions. The early Christians endured significantly more than we have.

Jesus died a horrible death on the cross. Paul was beaten, stoned, and imprisoned for preaching about the risen Christ. The New Testament only records the fates of Judas and James, but most of the apostles were martyred for their faith.

As Christians, we will suffer. We will be tested, and our faith will be tried. We can endure only by holding on to Him who gives the crown of life.

*As Christ suffered for us, O Lord,
give us courage to suffer for Him.*

AIMING TO PLEASE AND PRAISE

She said, "This time I'll praise GOD."
So she named him Judah (Praise-GOD).
GENESIS 29:35 MSG

Sometimes women get stressed out looking for love, recognition, contentment, and satisfaction in all the wrong places. Leah, knowing her husband, Jacob, had been tricked into marrying her, did all she could to win at least a portion of Jacob's love away from her barren sister, Rachel. Leah named her firstborn Reuben (*See, it's a boy!*), thinking that effort would make Jacob love her. The second she named Simeon, as she realized *God* had *heard* her prayers. The third she named Levi, *companion*, thinking now Jacob would connect with her. Finally, she had Judah, saying, "Now I'll *praise God*."

Amid our prayerful expectations, we would be wise to acknowledge, thank, and praise God for the comfort He continually gives us, even when our prayers are not answered exactly as we'd hoped, for the Lord alone should be the One we aim to please and praise in our lives.

I praise You, Lord, for all You have
done and are doing in my life!

UNFAMILIAR PATHS

I will lead the blind on unfamiliar roads. I will lead
them on unfamiliar paths. I will turn darkness into
light in front of them. I will make rough places smooth.
These are the things I will do for them,
and I will never abandon them.

ISAIAH 42:16 GW

Worrying about what may happen in the future, what to do in the present, or how to get over the past can make you feel as if you're blind, walking in the dark, lost and confused. Yet you need not worry about stumbling in the dark, unable to see the road ahead of you because God promises to lead you down unfamiliar paths. In fact, He'll transform the darkness into light right in front of your eyes! He'll make rocky places smooth. And He will never abandon you.

Because God promises that He'll always be with you, you can cease your worry and say with author Mary Gardiner Brainard, "I would rather walk with God in the dark than go alone in the light."

I'm with You, Lord, all the way!
Lead me down Your path, into Your light!

FEAR OF BETRAYAL

*And He answered, "He who dipped his hand with
Me in the bowl is the one who will betray Me."*
MATTHEW 26:23 NASB

Many of us bear invisible scars on our backs from the knives of false friends. The fear of betrayal can cripple our ability to trust others.

Considering Joseph, who suffered betrayal in the Bible, I searched for the reason God allowed it. Joseph's brothers betrayed him and he became the foreman of an estate in Egypt. Then his master's wife betrayed him, which led to him becoming second in command of all of Egypt.

Then I thought about what good came from my own incidents of being betrayed. A disloyal coworker pushed me to seek a higher-paying job. An unfaithful fiancé forced me to seek—and find—a godly man, who became my beloved husband.

Jesus knew that Judas Escariot would betray Him. Yet, trusting God's will, He understood the despicable act was necessary to bring about the crucifixion.

> *Dear God, as we endure the pain of betrayal,
> let us remember that we can always trust in
> You to bring about a good conclusion.*

FROM STRESS TO STRENGTH

*This is my prayer. That God. . .will give you spiritual
wisdom and the insight to know more of him: that you
may receive that inner illumination of the spirit which
will make you realise how great is the hope to which
he is calling you. . .and how tremendous is the
power available to us who believe in God.*

EPHESIANS 1:17–19 PHILLIPS

Within you lies all the power required to turn your stress
into strength and, in turn, turn your mourning into dancing
(see Psalm 30:11). But first you have to believe that the same
power that resurrected Jesus is alive and working in you! That
it's unlimited, unassailable, unbelievable!

Thousands of years ago, the apostle Paul prayed that God
would give you spiritual wisdom and insight to know Him
better and realize the amazing power available to you.

Look for it. Express it. Move out of your stress and into
God's strength—and dance.

*With Your Spirit within me, Lord, I can do all
You've called me to do. Keep this fact before
me as I move from stress to strength.*

GOD ONE STEP AHEAD

"I will answer them before they even call to me.
While they are still talking about their needs,
I will go ahead and answer their prayers!"
ISAIAH 65:24 NLT

How wonderful to have a God that answers you before you even cry out for Him! That while you're busy pouring out your worries, presenting God your what-if scenarios, and trying to put words to all you feel and are concerned about, He is already answering your petitions!

That's just who God is! That's just how much He cares about you! If you memorize today's verse and truly believe it, you can break up whatever worries come your way. You will trust the One who answers before you speak, the One who sees all the concerns, problems, and heartaches and is ready to soothe, solve, and salve.

Lord, I'm taking up my shield of faith in You,
knowing that You are already going before me,
answering my prayer, solving my problem, and
healing my heart. I praise Your name!

FEAR OF DECEPTION

*But I fear, lest somehow, as the serpent deceived Eve
by his craftiness, so your minds may be corrupted
from the simplicity that is in Christ.*

2 Corinthians 11:3 nkjv

The city of Corinth was known for rampant sin and idolatry, which concerned Paul. Would they be gullible to deceptive teachings?

Who is behind deception? What is the deceiver trying to hide from us? Why does he want to lead us astray? Where does he want to take us? When are we most susceptible to his trickery? How can we stand against this crafty adversary?

The serpent wants to conceal the truth about Christ's sacrifice. If we don't know what Jesus did for us, we can't share it with others. Bringing us to a state of confusion, he'll prod us to argue with each other instead of winning souls for God's kingdom. Misquoting God's Word, he tried to tempt Jesus when his body was weakened from fatigue, hunger, and thirst.

We can stand up to the deceiver through prayer and embracing God's Word.

*Holy God, when deception creeps in,
let the truth of Your Word banish it.*

MIND OF PLENTY

Every beast of the forest is Mine, and the cattle upon a thousand hills or upon the mountains where thousands are.

PSALM 50:10 AMPC

It's exhausting vying to buy the most and the best this world has to offer, all we think we are entitled to, trying to assuage the desperate feeling of not having enough. But this idea of lack is not put into us by God.

God constantly tells us of the plenty surrounding us. He knows exactly what we need and will provide it (see Matthew 6:25–33). Not that we aren't supposed to work. Even the apostle Paul was a tentmaker. The point is not to stress ourselves out trying to buy the most and the best. The point is to approach life with a mindset not of lack but of plenty, sharing what we have when we can (see Luke 3:11) and working with all our heart, as if we're working for the Lord (see Colossians 3:23), the One with cattle upon a thousand hills, knowing He will not fail to provide.

Lord, help me change my mindset from my lack to Your plenty.

MAKE UP YOUR MIND

*I have cheerfully made up my mind to be
proud of my weaknesses, because they mean a
deeper experience of the power of Christ. I can
even enjoy weaknesses, suffering, privations,
persecutions and difficulties for Christ's sake.
For my very weakness makes me strong in him.*

2 CORINTHIANS 12:10 PHILLIPS

God gives many gifts to His faithful followers, one of which
is that no matter how weak you are, no matter how much
you suffer or how often you worry, your very weaknesses give
Christ the chance to shine through you. For this formula to
work, though, you must have faith and then make up your
mind to live it.

God moves when you're truly helpless. He provides when
you have no more resources left. He will give you the power to
overcome all things—even worry. So revel in God, thanking
Him no matter what comes. He has all the strength you need
to triumph—to His glory!

*I've made up my mind, Lord! I'm going
to be content no matter what! In You
I have the strength to endure all!*

COURAGE TO KEEP SECRETS

He who goes about as a slanderer reveals secrets,
therefore do not associate with a gossip.
PROVERBS 20:19 NASB

How easily we get pulled into the feast of gossip. It starts with one tasty little tidbit that grows until our mouths water for more juicy details. Courage to change the subject or just walk away doesn't come easy. We must be prayerfully prepared.

Working for a government contractor many years ago taught me the benign reply to prying questions: "I can neither affirm nor deny any validity to that allegation." Nosy people tried to trip me up by making inaccurate statements about my work or fellow employees. I struggled to push away the bait of correcting them so I wouldn't appear ignorant. The World War II expression, "Loose lips sink ships," helped keep my mouth zipped.

We can apply the same attitude when faced with the temptation to gossip. The Lord doesn't want us to sabotage another human being.

Dear God, when others trust us with confidential details, give us the courage to embrace a new maxim: "I've got a secret, and the Lord will help me keep it."

FROM STRESS TO STILLNESS

*God did not give us a spirit of timidity (of cowardice,
of craven and cringing and fawning fear), but [He has
given us a spirit] of power and of love and of calm and
well-balanced mind and discipline and self-control.*

2 TIMOTHY 1:7 AMPC

Corrie ten Boom wrote, "Worry is a cycle of inefficient thoughts whirling around a center of fear." And once that whirling begins, it can grow to pull in every other thought that touches it, making your entire being spin out of control and be overtaken by stress.

The remedy is to remember God didn't give you a spirit of fear but of power, love, and calm. In Him your mind is well balanced. And as you become more aware of your thoughts, taking every one of them captive and turning them over to Christ, the waters settle. When we put God's truth up against the false worries that tend to drown us out, we find ourselves back with our Shepherd, beside the still waters.

*Thank You, Lord, for the spirit
of power and calm in You.*

GOD WALKS WITH YOU

*Yes, though I walk through the [deep, sunless] valley
of the shadow of death, I will fear or dread no evil,
for You are with me; Your rod [to protect] and
Your staff [to guide], they comfort me.*

PSALM 23:4 AMPC

God not only satisfies your basic human needs for food, water, warmth, and rest but also walks with you, equipped with two tools to make sure you're safe and heading the right way. He uses the first tool, His shepherd's rod, to stave off any force, power, or evil that threatens your life. He uses the second, His staff, to guide you through the shadows and onto the right path.

So the next time you're worried about your safety or where to take your next step, pray to God—the all-powerful Father and Shepherd who loves and adores you—remembering He's well equipped to protect you and more than ready to guide you.

*Lord, I feel Your presence by my side. With You
walking alongside me, I know I'll be safe
and heading down the right path.*

FEAR OF MORAL DECAY

The good influence of godly citizens causes a city to prosper,
but the moral decay of the wicked drives it downhill.

PROVERBS 11:11 TLB

Every generation since God wrote and gave His laws to Moses has chipped away at the foundation of His laws. We've seen the pendulum of morality swing back and forth over thousands of years of human history.

In today's society, people scoff at the concept of purity in mind and body. Standing firm in our ethical convictions brings us under scrutiny and ridicule. Unbelievers wait with bated breath for us to fall into a pit of sin.

Living under their vigilant appraisals, our attitudes, words, and actions could be an influence of integrity to those around us. When we pray, let us show our joy when God answers—even for His "no" responses. When frustration comes upon us, we can show our trust in God, proclaiming He is in control. Tempted to gossip? Ask the Lord to close your mouth.

Righteous God, give us courage to influence people
in our midst to come to know and trust in You.

CHANGE YOUR OUTLOOK

*Jesus called a little child to his side. . . . "Believe me,"
he said, "unless you change your whole outlook
and become like little children you will never
enter the kingdom of Heaven."*
MATTHEW 18:2–3 PHILLIPS

Take this moment to check in with yourself. What's your outlook? Are you seeing this world as a hard place to exist, wondering when the next proverbial shoe will drop? Are you expecting the clouds instead of the sun?

Imagine being a small, innocent child with no agenda, one who trusts, loves, forgives easily, and has no ego. Imagine holding Jesus' hand, knowing He's your big brother, the One who will keep you safe, feed you, lead you, help you, lift you up. As you hold on to His hand, imagine walking by His side. The world is a wonderland as you walk through it, curious as to what you will find, what gifts you will uncover.

Hold on to that hand. Change your outlook. Become God's child.

*God of my heart and soul, hold my hand.
Lead me. I am but Your child.*

ASLEEP AND AWAKE IN GOD

When you go, they [the words of your parents' God]
shall lead you; when you sleep, they shall keep you;
and when you waken, they shall talk with you.
PROVERBS 6:22 AMPC

Some people's parents make it a point to make sure their children are versed in God's power-filled words. Other parents don't, but hopefully a child will end up learning God's wisdom through "spiritual" parents. Either way, knowing God's Word and following it can keep you, Father God's child, from letting your worries careen out of control.

Wherever you go, allow God's Word to lead you down the right path. While you sleep, allow it to comfort and protect you. And when you wake, seek God's Word through reading, His voice through prayer, allowing both to talk to you, giving you all the wisdom you need to keep from stumbling, to make the choices God would have you make throughout your day.

Heavenly Father, help me to lean heavily on Your Word.
Talk to me, guide me, comfort and protect me.

COURAGE TO FIGHT FOR OUR FAITH

"Do not be afraid of them; remember the Lord who is great and awesome, and fight for your brothers, your sons, your daughters, your wives and your houses."

NEHEMIAH 4:14 NASB

Sanballat the Horonite, Tobiah the Ammonite, and Geshem the Arab conspired to attack the laborers on the Jerusalem wall.

Nehemiah prayed and assigned guards to protect the workers and the wall.

God answered by thwarting the attackers' plans.

The builders continued their work with a tool in one hand and a sword in the other.

Today, we face similar assaults against our faith. But our attackers come through the courts, legislators, and mass media. They pervert the law to demoralize our workers.

Fierce battles are necessary when our faith is challenged. Let us continue our Christian duties with our everyday tools in one hand, and the sword of the Lord in the other. We must protect our freedom of religion for the sake of those who follow behind us.

Hear, O God, our prayer. We need Your help in this fight for our brothers, our sons, our daughters, our spouses, and our homes.

WALKING IN RHYTHM

"May GOD, our very own God. . .keep us centered and devoted to him, following the life path he has cleared, watching the signposts, walking at the pace and rhythms he laid down for our ancestors."
1 KINGS 8:57–58 MSG

When we are walking out of step with God, stress can seep into our lives. Where might you be off center? How might you have stepped off the path God has laid out for you? What distractions have kept you from watching for, seeing, reading the signposts He has planted for you throughout your journey? How can you get out of the rhythm of this walk you have set out on and get back to God's pace for your life?

Spend some time taking an inventory of your activities, priorities, goals. Go to God in prayer and ask where your priorities might differ from His. Then begin revising your stride to keep pace with His rhythm on His good path.

Lord, I come to You, looking to set my pace with Yours.

WHAT'S IN YOUR HAND?

*Moses answered, But behold, they will not believe me or
listen to and obey my voice; for they will say, The Lord
has not appeared to you. And the Lord said to him,
What is that in your hand? And he said, A rod.*

EXODUS 4:1–2 AMPC

So God has called you and, like Moses, you still have worries, self-doubts. That's when God calls your attention to the tools you already have, the ones you're very familiar with, the ones in your hand or your company.

For Moses, one tool was his shepherd's staff, which he'd later use to part waters, lead people, strike rocks, turn rivers to blood. Your tool might be your pen, voice, talent, vehicle, knitting needle. Another of Moses' tools was his brother, Aaron, one who could speak well.

Instead of worrying about how you'll do something, look to see what you have in your hand or who you have at your side. Pray for God to reveal your tools, and then use them.

*What, Lord, would You have me use to serve You?
Reveal my tools for Your glory!*

FEAR OF SUCCESS

*And the Lord replied, "I myself will go
with you and give you success."*
EXODUS 33:14 TLB

We hide behind the door when opportunity knocks, afraid to answer.

Self-doubt of our inner strengths holds us back. Will we trade our moral values for success? Will we arrogantly flaunt our success to those trailing behind us?

We lack confidence in our skills. Or we could be sure of our abilities, but not our motives.

Success usually means a new direction in life. Will we have to leave family, friends, and familiar territory?

All of these questions went through my mind as I sabotaged my brief acting career in my thirties. I answered them with other questions: Is this what God wants for me? Could I honor Him in my self-centered performing arts profession? Through my spiritual growth and study of the Bible, I can now rejoice in the new success He has provided to bring Him glory.

*Dear God, let Moses' words be ours when faced
with our fears of success: If Your presence does
not go with us, do not lead us up from here.*

RECOGNITION

Now when they saw the boldness of Peter and John, and perceived that they were uneducated, common men, they were astonished. And they recognized that they had been with Jesus.

ACTS 4:13 ESV

Sometimes the symptoms of stress can be quite obvious—low energy, nervousness, loss of focus, sleeplessness, weakness, timidity, jumpiness, tenseness, etc.—all of which keep others (and ourselves, perhaps) from recognizing that we have been with Jesus. For His persona exudes the exact opposite characteristics. Jesus is tireless, calm, focused, rested, bold, peaceful, and relaxed.

Spend time each day with Jesus. When you do, His characteristics will rub off on you bit by bit. Each day you will become more like Him until one day, people will look at you and recognize you have spent time in the presence of Jesus.

At this point, Jesus, I'm not sure what—or who people see when they look at me. So I'm coming to spend time with You, imbibing Your peace, strength, boldness, and so much more. May I grow each day to look more like You than anything or anyone else.

ALL IS WELL

She said, "All is well."
2 KINGS 4:23 ESV

A childless woman went out of her way to provide a room where Elisha, a man of God, could rest when he came into town. To repay her, Elisha told her she'd have a baby. And she did. A boy. But then he died. So she laid her son on Elisha's bed and went to find Elisha. When her husband asked why she was going out, she simply said, "All is well." She repeated the phrase to Elisha's servant, who, seeing her coming, asked if anything was wrong (see 2 Kings 4:26). And in the end, all *was* well, for Elisha brought the boy back to life.

Imagine what would've happened if she'd been paralyzed by worry. If she'd kept repeating, "All is wrong." The point? Go the way of this woman. No matter what's happening, know God has a plan. Somehow, He'll make everything turn out right.

Lord, I know You make all things work out to Your good. Help me adopt the mantra that no matter what things look like to me, all is well in You.

COURAGE TO FAIL

The Ten Commandments were given so that all could see
the extent of their failure to obey God's laws.
ROMANS 5:20 TLB

Peter, the apostle of Jesus Christ, tried, but failed to remain obedient to the Lord. He slept while Jesus prayed, he cut off a soldier's ear, and then he denied Christ three times.

We are flawed human beings, unable to yield our will to God's standard every day. Our imperfections prove that we can never be good enough to come to the Lord on our own. When we fail to follow His way, God's grace encourages us to get back in step again.

Like Peter, we will encounter failures along our Christian path. The Lord gives us the courage to overcome them so we can continue to grow in our faith, as He did for Peter.

God provided a standard to measure our obedience—the Ten Commandments. He didn't set us up to fail by creating an unreachable goal; He showed us we need Christ, the Savior, the fulfillment of the Law.

Heavenly Father, our failures weighed
against Your commandments attest to
Your abounding grace and forgiveness.

HER PART, HIS PART

*"Now, Lord. . .grant to your servants to continue to
speak your word with all boldness, while you stretch out
your hand to heal, and signs and wonders are performed
through the name of your holy servant Jesus." And when
they had prayed. . .they were all filled with the Holy Spirit
and continued to speak the word of God with boldness.*
ACTS 4:29–31 ESV

Feeling as if the whole world is on your shoulders? Thinking if
you don't do it, it won't get done? Stop and consider that those
feelings and thoughts are lies. For you have a God who is in it
with you all the way. In fact, He wants you to know there are
two parts to consider in your life—yours and His.

Your part is to immerse yourself in God's Word, pray, welcome His Spirit, expect the Lord is acting on your behalf, and
leave the results to Him. His part is to work wonders.

*Lord, help me to do what You would
have me do and leave the rest to You.*

WATCH AND WAIT

In the morning You hear my voice, O Lord; in the
morning I prepare [a prayer, a sacrifice] for You and
watch and wait [for You to speak to my heart].
PSALM 5:3 AMPC

One of the best places to have a Bible is right by your bed, for then you can connect with God before your feet even hit the floor. To help you springboard into this idea of making reading the Word a morning habit, begin by reading the psalms, specifically Psalm 5:3.

It acknowledges that God hears your voice in the morning as you prepare a prayer for Him. It reminds you not to just read some words and then jump out of bed, but to pray "and watch and wait" for God to speak to your heart. To give you the exact words that will keep your mind free from worry, give your soul peace, and calm your spirit.

In the morning You hear my voice, O Lord; in this
moment I prepare a prayer for You. And now I
watch and wait for You to speak into my heart.

FEAR OF POVERTY

"For the poor will never cease to be in the land; therefore
I command you, saying, 'You shall freely open your hand
to your brother, to your needy and poor in your land.' "

DEUTERONOMY 15:11 NASB

Poverty results from either financial judgment errors, or circumstances beyond our control. Sometimes we just can't get ahead. Job loss, auto repairs, medical costs, taxes, and fees all mount up against us.

Our fears grow like strangling weeds when we are unable to provide for our families. So we look for relief in high-interest loans, credit card advances, or gambling—and losing. Worldly solutions only serve to worsen our situations.

When we look to the Lord, praying with expectation, He will answer. Trusting Him for our sustenance opens wide the door to His supply.

The Lord didn't merely encourage charitable giving; He commanded it. And as such, He will use others in our godly family to provide assistance. They'll come with job offers, financial gifts, and groceries.

And His love.

Loving Father, give hope and courage to
our brethren who live in poverty today.
Show us how we can help them.

Day 170
NO DISTRACTIONS

*Josiah. . .began his thirty-one-year reign
in Jerusalem. . . . He did right in the
sight of the Lord. . .and turned not aside
to the right hand or to the left.*
2 KINGS 22:1–2 AMPC

Josiah was one of the best kings of Judah because he did not allow himself to turn aside from God's calling on his life.

When we're moving along on the path God has called us to, it's easy to get distracted by things along the way. When we do, we begin losing ground on what we're supposed to be doing, where we're supposed to be going. Falling ever further behind, we feel the stress of not being where we're supposed to be, and it begins to overwhelm us.

Look to what may be in your path. Then consider living by the wisdom of Proverbs 4:25–27: "Keep your eyes straight ahead; ignore all sideshow distractions. Watch your step, and the road will stretch out smooth before you. Look neither right nor left" (MSG).

*Help me steer clear of distractions, Lord,
and keep my feet firmly on Your path.*

GOD'S SHIELD OF LOVE

For You, Lord, will bless the [uncompromisingly]
righteous [him who is upright and in right standing
with You]; as with a shield You will surround him
with goodwill (pleasure and favor).

PSALM 5:12 AMPC

When you begin seeking God early, expecting Him to speak to your heart, taking refuge in and trusting Him (see Psalm 5:3, 11), not only will your worries take a backseat to God's presence in your life, but He will bless you in so many other ways! He will show you the way to walk and talk. He'll clear the path before you, be with you just where you are, and watch your back from behind. He will surround you with His shield of love and bless you with His favor!

As your worries fall like scales from your eyes, you will be able to see all God is doing in your life, all the blessings He is putting in your path. Your life will be full of pleasure behind God's shield of abundant love.

Lord, surround me with Your shield of love so
that my eyes may see Your blessings in my life.

FEAR OF FINANCIAL RUIN

*But those who want to get rich fall
into temptation and a snare.*
1 TIMOTHY 6:9 NASB

Many foolish and harmful desires plunge men and women into ruin and destruction. Does anyone, besides the vendor, ever get wealthy from a get rich quick scheme? Selling instructional books or CDs is part of the marketing plan. The coaching materials usually collect dust on a shelf when they don't produce the desired results.

The threat of financial ruin is almost always the conduit that draws desperate people to the brokers of these schemes. The "low risk / high return" plans sound inviting. An occasional small gain persuades the investor to contribute more, only to get caught up in the trap of losing their initial capital. The financial ruin they feared will fall on them like an avalanche.

The best investment we can make when our financial failures seem imminent is in the Lord. He knows our situation.

*Father God, give us discernment to be good stewards
with our money and the courage to trust You
to carry us through financial ruin.*

TIDES OF THE MIND

Now ask and keep on asking and you will receive, so that
your joy (gladness, delight) may be full and complete.
JOHN 16:24 AMPC

Poet and suffragist Alice Meynell wrote, "Happiness is not a matter of events; it depends upon the tides of the mind." If you've been looking for happiness in other people or circumstances to no avail, Jesus has your answer. He can help you to have joy in any situation if you simply ask Him to help you navigate the tides of your mind, keeping life events from becoming major stressors.

If you miss the bus, send up a prayer, then look around to see what God might want you to do. Perhaps you now have time for devotions, could help a fellow traveler get a coffee, or could give your warm scarf to a homeless person. In other words, find your joy in every life event. See every event and seeming setback as neither good nor bad but rather as a chance to pray and see the opportunity God is presenting you.

Control the tides of my mind, Lord,
so my joy will be in You alone.

PREVAIL IN PROMISES

"Don't worry about a thing. Go ahead and do what you've said. But first make a small biscuit for me and bring it back here. Then go ahead and make a meal from what's left for you and your son."
1 KINGS 17:13 MSG

The prophet Elijah approached a poor widow gathering firewood. He asked her to bring him water and something to eat. She told him all she had left was "a handful of flour in a jar and a little oil in a bottle," just enough to "make a last meal" for herself and her son (1 Kings 17:12 MSG).

But Elisha told her not to worry, that God promised her oil and flour would not run out before God sent rain to end the drought. Hearing those words, the widow put aside her worries, waved off her parental instincts, and obeyed Elijah. For the next two years, God provided as promised.

Have faith. God will provide as promised.

Lord, I never want my faith to run dry.
I believe in You and Your promises!

COURAGE IN TRIUMPH

*For whatever is born of God overcomes the
world. And this is the victory that has overcome
the world—our faith.*

1 JOHN 5:4 NKJV

Corrie ten Boom said, "The first step on the way to victory is
to recognize the enemy."

In today's world, how do we recognize our enemy? He doesn't
wear a shirt with ENEMY emblazoned across the front. I've never
seen "*I am your enemy—Hire me*" typed on a business card.

The Bible clearly reveals our foes in Matthew 12:30 (NKJV)
when Jesus told the Pharisees, "He who is not with Me is against
Me." This describes most of the world. A force that large could
be frightening. But John reminds us that we have victory over
the world through Jesus Christ.

Protected by her shield of faith, Corrie triumphed over the
enemy with her Christian faith before, during, and after her
imprisonment.

Like Corrie, we celebrate a successful coup d'état with every
new believer we bring into the family of God.

*Lord, thank You for Corrie ten Boom,
who identified Your enemies and, in faith,
claimed victory over them.*

A MATTER OF COURSE

*"So don't worry and don't keep saying, 'What shall
we eat. . .drink or. . .wear?' . . . Set your heart on
the kingdom and his goodness, and all these things
will come to you as a matter of course."*
MATTHEW 6:31, 33 PHILLIPS

So many people are stressed out because they put more value and priority on those things that give them a monetary reward. In other words, they put work before time with relatives, children, spouses, friends—even God. They have, as playwright Arthur Miller put it, been "seduced into thinking that that which does not make a profit is without value."

Jesus tells us that the most valuable thing we can do is seek Him and His kingdom above all else. Then we will be given all those other things we need. Consider your priorities today. Have you made time for God, secure in the knowledge that everything else will fall into place once He's number one in your life?

*Lord, I'm here, seeking You above all else.
My new course is to set my heart on You.*

BEDTIME PRAYER

In peace I will both lie down and sleep, for You, Lord,
alone make me dwell in safety and confident trust.
PSALM 4:8 AMPC

King David, the author of today's psalm, had surely had his share of challenges. As a shepherd boy, he'd had to fight lions and bears to keep his father's sheep safe. Later he'd faced a giant, been chased by King Saul, was betrayed by his son Absalom, and fought countless battles.

You too have lots of challenges. Yet you have a God-Father-King-Shepherd you can run to. One who has rescued, encouraged, provided for, and fought for you time after time. He's answered your prayers, has loved you like no other, has gifted you with eternal life, and has made you, His daughter, a princess. You can count on Him to keep you safe, to watch over you.

So when your head hits the pillow, override your worries with God's Word. Bring today's verse to mind. Repeat it slowly, absorbing its power, and you will find the peace you need for a good night's sleep.

In You, loving Lord, I find the peace to sleep,
for You alone keep me safe and sound.

FEAR OF WARS

*"You will be hearing of wars and rumors of wars.
See that you are not frightened, for those things
must take place, but that is not yet the end."*
MATTHEW 24:6 NASB

The first war in history occurred between two men: Cain and Abel. Since then, bitter conflicts have one trait in common: covetousness. Someone wants what the other has.

An assassination started World War I—the proposed war to end all wars. The Treaty of Versailles brought it to a close. That pact severely punished Germany. Rebellion against the treaty's restrictions brought about World War II. When that conflict ended, hostilities persisted—not only in battlefields but also in a cold war of suspicious envy.

Will we ever see the end of wars? The book of Revelation describes the fulfillment of Christ's prediction. The last battle ends Satan's hold on us. When he is cast away for eternity, the curse of covetousness will go with him.

Dear God, thank You for providing this glimpse of future peace. We take courage in the truth that You will be victorious in the indisputable "War to End All Wars."

IMPRINT ON CHRIST

Throw off your old sinful nature and your former way of life, which is corrupted by lust and deception. Instead, let the Spirit renew your thoughts and attitudes. Put on your new nature, created to be like God—truly righteous and holy.

Ephesians 4:22–24 nlt

Newly hatched birds follow the first moving thing they see, thinking it's their mother. This process is called imprinting. And it's the same process that you, a new creature in Christ, should be following. Now that your spirit has been reborn, now that you have a new nature, you are not to stress out while living in this world but to let God's Spirit renew your mindset as you follow Jesus.

Throw off the angst and put on Christ's peace. Let go of sorrow and reach out for His joy. Look away from your lack and focus on His abundance. Release all doubts and cling to your faith. Exchange your impatience with His patience. Erase all stress as you imprint on Christ.

You, Jesus, are my Brother. May I become more and more like You every day.

PRAYING FOR ALL

I admonish and urge that petitions, prayers, intercessions, and thanksgivings be offered on behalf of all men. . .that [outwardly] we may pass a quiet and undisturbed life [and inwardly] a peaceable one in all godliness and reverence and seriousness in every way.
1 TIMOTHY 2:1–2 AMPC

There may be some people in positions of power or authority with whom you disagree or feel uncomfortable. There may be some you think will lead your town, city, state, or country down the wrong road. You worry that they don't have the best interests of you and other people at heart.

Rather than worry about what leaders may or may not do next, the apostle Paul urges you to go to God. To pray for "kings and all who are in positions of authority or high responsibility" (see 1 Timothy 2:2 AMPC). For that's the only way you'll be able to live in peace—within and without.

I want to pray for all people in all positions, Lord. Help me pray for our leaders so that I can gain Your blessing of true peace within and without.

FEAR OF PEACE

*"Peace I leave with you, My peace I give to you;
not as the world gives do I give to you. Let not your
heart be troubled, neither let it be afraid."*

JOHN 14:27 NKJV

Peace is defined as the absence of war or strife, a state of calm. Yet a season of peace can be frightening. We miss the calm before the storm while watching for thunderclouds of distress. Our joy of peace is lost in constantly looking over our shoulders and asking, "Will they attack today?"

There will be another attack, another battle, and another war. Peace has been short-lived since evil entered the world.

Christ offers us the calmness of spirit that comes only through Him. The world offers moments of tranquility, but His gift of peace is eternal. Our hearts are free from trouble when we keep our focus on the Lord. With Jesus as our ally, why would we fear the calm before the storm? We know true peace in the presence of our Savior.

*Father God, we seek Your peace every day so
our hearts will not be troubled, nor afraid.*

THE HEALING WORD

*My child, pay attention to what I say. Listen carefully to
my words. Don't lose sight of them. Let them penetrate
deep into your heart, for they bring life to those who
find them, and healing to their whole body.*
PROVERBS 4:20–22 NLT

Too much stress, worry, and strain can cause you physical
damage, not to mention emotional, psychological, mental, and
spiritual harm. But God's Word can heal all that.

Make it a daily endeavor to delve into God's Word. If you
have a good half hour, soak in His wisdom. If you have less
than that, even only one minute, ask God to show you what
He would have you know today. Then open your Bible or
devotional. Uncover a verse that speaks to you. Focus on its
content, intent, and portent. Ask God how it applies to your
life, and acknowledge that it's feeding and healing your whole
self, leading you from feeling stressed to feeling blessed.

*Thank You, God, for feeding me, healing
me with the power of Your Word.*

A HEART-TO-HEART ATTITUDE

When Solomon finished making these prayers and petitions to the LORD, he stood up in front of the altar of the LORD, where he had been kneeling with his hands raised toward heaven.

1 KINGS 8:54 NLT

Prayer is a form of worship, and everyone has their own prayer posture. Some pray with eyes closed, hands folded, or head bowed. King Solomon kneeled and raised his hands toward heaven.

The point is to not judge how other people pray or worry about what others may say about how *you* pray. As the Reverend Billy Graham said, "It's not the body's posture but the heart's attitude that counts when we pray."

Jesus told the woman at the well, "It's who you are and the way you live that count before God. Your worship must engage your spirit in the pursuit of truth. That's the kind of people the Father is out looking for: those who are simply and honestly themselves before him in their worship" (John 4:23 MSG).

Today, go before God for a heart-to-heart talk, conscious of your own heart attitude. Look for places where you might need to be more of who you truly are as you come before God.

Here I am, Lord, coming before You, just as I am.

OUR WOBBLING WORLD

God is our refuge and strength, a very present help in trouble. Therefore we will not fear, though the earth should change and though the mountains slip into the heart of the sea.

PSALM 46:1–2 NASB

Japanese engineers created a twenty-foot-high wall on the coast to protect them from imminent tsunamis. An earthquake opened a cavern under the sea, which dropped the shoreline approximately twenty feet. The ensuing tidal wave rushed far into the countryside, mocking their human efforts.

A volcano erupted in Europe, halting air transportation for days. Toxic clouds mingled with the weather pattern, making it too dangerous for airplanes to fly. Tourists and business travelers found themselves stranded in foreign countries.

The psalmist states that God is a very "present" help, which means He is always here to care for us, especially during earthquakes, tsunamis, and volcanic eruptions.

Dear Lord, You warned us that these geological instabilities would increase in volume and intensity as the earth begins to writhe in birth pains. By Your Word we know that You are our refuge and strength. Let us look to You with hope and not fear.

FAITHFUL INVESTMENT

*" 'Well done!' the king exclaimed. 'You are
a good servant. You have been faithful
with the little I entrusted to you.' "*

LUKE 19:17 NLT

Before going on a long trip, a nobleman divides ten pounds of silver between three servants, saying, "Invest this for me while I am gone" (verse 13 NLT). When the nobleman returns as king, the first servant reports he invested his portion of the master's money and increased it tenfold. The second says his investment increased fivefold. Both of these servants are rewarded according to how they profited. But the last servant, who, fearing the master, did nothing but hid his master's money to keep it safe, is stripped of what he was given.

The point is that God wants you to invest the gifts He's given you but not stress over the results. Your responsibility is to do only what He asks. Then relax, leaving the results to Him, and return for further orders, rejoicing over a task completed in His name.

*Lord, show me how to invest the gifts You've
given me then leave the results to You alone.*

YOUR BURDEN BEARER, DAY BY DAY

Blessed be the Lord, Who bears our burdens and carries us day by day, even the God Who is our salvation! Selah [pause, and calmly think of that]!
PSALM 68:19 AMPC

How blessed you are to have a God who loves you so much He will not only bear your burdens but will carry you! And not just once but every single day! Knowing and truly believing this, living as if it is true (which it is), gives you the peace of mind, heart, body, and spirit you need to live a fabulous life, free of worry! Yet the benefits don't stop there. Along with God bearing your load, He's decided you will be strong!

Today give God your worries. Believe that He's carrying them—and you. Then enter your day in the strength He gives you.

Lord, my worries have been weighing me down. Thank You so much for carrying them—and me—today and every day. Such knowledge gives me the strength I need.

COURAGE IN GLOBAL TRIBULATIONS

*"These things I have spoken to you, so that in Me you
may have peace. In the world you have tribulation,
but take courage; I have overcome the world."*
JOHN 16:33 NASB

Explosions rip apart cities. Terrorist groups claim responsibility, hiding like cowards behind obscurity.

Bands of angry rebels use deadly force in their failed coup attempts.

A worldwide financial meltdown looms in the shadow of national monetary collapses.

These represent a few "breaking news" stories that invade our homes every day.

These global tribulations could cause us to wring our hands in anguish, but Jesus didn't call us to live in fear. When we view these trials through His eyes, our hearts break for those who live in terror and hopelessness. We all have resources to help those in need to rebuild, if not physically and emotionally, then in sharing Christ's love. Even when our only recourse is to turn to the Lord in prayer, we find courage through our faith in Him.

*Father God, fortify us as we kneel before
You in prayer. We know You have
conquered the evils of this world.*

UNDER THE INFLUENCE

*"Teacher," they said, "we know that you speak and teach
what is right and are not influenced by what others
think. You teach the way of God truthfully."*
LUKE 20:21 NLT

Pastor Harry Emerson Fosdick said, "Prayer is putting yourself under God's influence." To understand this and the above verse better, let's look at the etymology of the word *influence*. According to etymonline.com, *influence* is a late-fourteenth-century astrological term, meaning "streaming ethereal power from the stars when in certain positions, acting upon the character or destiny of men" and also "a flow of water, flowing in."

Stop for a moment. Ask yourself whose influence you are under during most of your day. Then consider how you can put yourself under *God's* influence 24–7 through prayer. Doing so will keep you from bowing to the influence of society, the media, and so on, and keep your pathway to peace secure.

*I'm tired of worrying about what other people
think about who I am, what I do. I want You,
Lord, to be my one and only influence.
Stream Your guiding Spirit upon me.*

BE STILL

God is in the midst of her; she shall not be moved;
God will help her when morning dawns.
PSALM 46:5 ESV

No matter what troubles you're facing or what worries are upon your mind, you have a mighty fortress in God. He's your "refuge and strength, an ever-present help in times of trouble" (Psalm 46:1 GW). Because He is living within you and you're abiding in Him, you cannot be harmed or moved. He brings His full power, all His angels, all His resources, visible and invisible, material and temporal, to aid you. He shields, empowers, and frees you.

God brings His peace to you, telling you, gently, "I've got this. You need not worry." He tells you your role in all this. It's to simply "let be and be still, and know (recognize and understand) that I am God" (Psalm 46:10 AMPC).

Today, make it your aim to let be and be still. Know your God is taking care of everything. He's got this.

Oh Lord, help me understand You better. Help me
to be still, to let all things be, to let You take
care of everything—including me.

FEARING THE END OF THE WORLD

"Heaven and earth will pass away, but My
words will by no means pass away."
MATTHEW 24:35 NKJV

The end will come. The Lord Jesus Christ predicted it. Every generation since His ascension has asked in fear, "Is the end really near?"

Only God knows the precise time it will occur. In His mercy, the Creator has hidden it from us. He knows we mortals tend to procrastinate, and then panic.

Jesus provided advance warning in the scriptures. First, false prophets will claim to be Christ, misleading many. We will hear of wars and rumors of wars. Nations will come against nations. Then famines and earthquakes will increase. Knowing these are only the beginning of the end is frightening. How much worse could it get?

We can conquer our fears of the end by holding on to the words of Jesus—words that will never pass away.

O God our Creator, You have given us time to
prepare our hearts for the end. Let us use it wisely
to share the Gospel of the kingdom with the
whole world, one person at a time.

THE QUIET POWER OF WOMEN

In quietness and in [trusting]
confidence shall be your strength.
ISAIAH 30:15 AMPC

In the British television series *Wycliffe*, Detective Superintendent Charles Wycliffe remarks to his wife, "It's interesting, isn't it, the quiet power of women." That statement is just as true today as it was thousands of years ago.

Consider the fact that men have most of the lines in the Bible. Yet most women, when they do speak, do so with passion and power. Esther suggested a fast for her people then simply said, "If I perish, I perish" (Esther 4:16 ESV). The woman with the issue of blood thought (but did not say), "If I can just touch his robe, I will be healed" (Mark 5:28 NLT). The women standing at the cross said. . .nothing. And in the garden, when Mary Magdalene realized the supposed gardener was actually Jesus, she said simply, "Teacher!" and then ran to tell the others the good news.

Don't stress. You have a quiet power. Prayer is a part of that power. Stress less, pray more.

Lord, may my confidence in You
be my source of quiet power.

COME AWAY WITH GOD

His left hand is under my head, and his right hand
embraces me! . . . My beloved speaks and says to me:
"Arise, my love, my beautiful one, and come away."
SONG OF SONGS 2:6, 10 ESV

God longs to have an intimate relationship with you. He doesn't want your worries about what may or may not happen to become a barrier between you, to distract you from what He can do and is doing in your life.

To tear down the wall of worry, find a quiet place. Tell God all that's on your mind. Relax as you imagine God right next to you. Say, "[I can feel] his left hand under my head and his right hand embraces me!" (Song of Songs 2:6 AMPC). Spend as much time as you'd like with Him, enjoying His presence, listening for His voice, hearing what He has to say. Then arise, beautiful one, and go with Him wherever He leads.

I can feel Your left hand beneath my head,
Your right hand embracing me. Let me rest in
this peace, surrounded by Your presence and love.

COURAGE TO FACE TODAY

*Wail, for the day of the LORD is near! It will
come as destruction from the Almighty.*
ISAIAH 13:6 NASB

Today terrorists will choose new targets. They'll attack in the middle of the night, the middle of the day, the middle of a parade, or the middle of a race. But always in muddled secrecy.

Reports of violence come at us through mass media, including the internet, not just daily, but minute by minute. Yet, if we look beyond the reports, we can find order in the chaos. Isaiah, among other prophets, warned of the great and terrible day of the Lord. As their prophecies unfold before us, let us look to the future day with courage.

"And Jesus said to him, 'Assuredly, I say to you, today you will be with Me in Paradise'" (Luke 23:43 NKJV). Since we have Christ our Savior, we have no reason to fear the predicted day of the Lord's judgment. Like the thief on the cross next to Jesus, we will be with Him in paradise.

*Let today be the day, we pray, O Lord.
Let it be today.*

CHANGE AGENT

Be careful how you live. . . . Make the most of every opportunity. . . . Don't act thoughtlessly, but understand what the Lord wants you to do. . . . Be filled with the Holy Spirit. . .making music to the Lord in your hearts.

Ephesians 5:15–19 nlt

Want to have some change in your life, live more in God's world than the one you've created for yourself? Tap into the power of the Holy Spirit. He's the change agent who will bring you around to where God desires you to be. He's as close as a breath, as near as a prayer. He's the gift of the One who loved you so much He died for you on the cross.

He's not only your Comforter, Counselor, Motivator, and Life Source. He's the One who'll change your attitude (see Romans 12:2) and your altitude, drawing you ever closer to the God of your heart, mind, body, and soul.

Lord, I'm ready for a change in my life. Help me to handle it, drawing ever closer to You in the process.

THE MASTER PLANNER

*We are God's [own] handiwork. . .recreated in Christ
Jesus. . .that we may do those good works which God
predestined (planned beforehand) for us [taking paths
which He prepared ahead of time], that we should
walk in them [. . .for us to live].*

EPHESIANS 2:10 AMPC

God, the Master Planner, had you in mind before time began,
designed you, then re-created you in Christ so you could be a
part of His grand plan. He has paths He's prepared for you to
take, all so you could live the good life He made ready for you.
But how can you do all God has planned, live the amazing life
He's carved out, if you're saddled by worry?

You're in God's plan, but your worries are not. So stop
wringing your hands. Give God all you can't handle, and settle
down in His peace. Live "the good life which He prearranged
and made ready" for you to live.

*Lord, I'm amazed at the plans You've made for me.
Help me leave my worries behind, settle into Your
peace, and walk down the path You've laid out.*

COURAGE IN THE EYE OF THE STORM

But when he saw that the wind was
boisterous, he was afraid; and beginning to
sink he cried out, saying, "Lord, save me!"
MATTHEW 14:30 NKJV

Aside from the obvious: wind, lightning, thunder, and precipitation, stormy weather can also represent looming ominous conditions.

Jesus knew His disciples would run into a storm when He ordered them across the Sea of Galilee. He also knew that persecution hung over their future ministry.

As Jesus approached them on the stormy sea, only Peter had the courage to get out of the boat. By faith, he could walk on water—not calm, smooth-as-glass water, but rising waves from tempestuous winds. Peter sank when he allowed his surroundings to distract him. He cried out to the Lord, and Jesus saved him.

In calming the storm, Jesus taught the disciples who He was, is, and ever shall be. This lesson in faith prepared them for the assaults they would face, even after Jesus' death, resurrection, and ascension. Let it prepare us too.

Dear God, grant us courage to call on You
in faith as we tread our stormy seas.

SLOW AND STEADY

*The thoughts of the [steadily] diligent tend only
to plenteousness, but everyone who is impatient
and hasty hastens only to want.*
PROVERBS 21:5 AMPC

How many times have you felt stressed out because your boss
said she needed that report yesterday? How many days a week
do you speed from one kid's activity to another then rush home
to get dinner on before hubby gets home? How many times have
you taken what seemed to be a shortcut but found it actually
took you longer to reach your destination?

God wants all things we do to be done in His time, in His
rhythm. Proverbs 21:5 (NLT) says that "hasty shortcuts lead
to poverty." How can we have a good walk with Jesus if we're
always struggling in the yoke that binds us to Him?

First, change your thoughts. Know that God will help you
do what needs to be done each day, and the rest will wait. Slow
and steady will win the race.

*Lord, help me to slow down in my thoughts
and actions, knowing all things will
get done in Your time.*

NIGHT WATCHES

When I remember You upon my bed and meditate on
You in the night watches. For You have been my help,
and in the shadow of Your wings will I rejoice.
My whole being follows hard after You and clings
closely to You; Your right hand upholds me.
PSALM 63:6–8 AMPC

It's late at night, and you should be fast asleep. But for some reason, you're still awake. In the quiet darkness, it's easy to let your mind wander into the even darker territory of worry. But why not switch up your thought pattern and go from worry to wonder by meditating on God.

Remember how much God has done for you. How He protected and cared for you, helped you, and provided all you needed to make it to this point in your day and in your life. Rejoice in and thank Him for all the blessings He has bestowed upon you. Then see yourself clinging to Him as He holds you up, carries you, and pours out upon you His strength and peace.

Hold me, Lord, as I cling to You,
absorbing Your presence and peace.

FEARING SPIRITUAL WARFARE

*"Then Michael, one of the top officers of the heavenly
army, came to help me, so that I was able to break
through these spirit rulers of Persia."*
DANIEL 10:13 TLB

Our earthly wars cannot compare to the combat raging in
the spirit world. A twenty-one-day struggle delayed the angel
responding to Daniel's prayer. That angel enlisted Michael's
help to overcome his evil opponents.

The devil and his demons gave up their home in heaven
when they dissented against God. Satan appears to be stepping
up the pace of his vile attacks because he knows his period of
influence is growing shorter.

We catch an occasional glimpse of his warfare if we pay
close attention to fearful events—from worldwide tensions to
family conflicts. But the apostle John's vision of the battle in
Revelation 12 gives us courage. We know the Victor of that
war. Our Father's goodness always triumphs over evil.

*Dear God, we know by Your Word that we need not
fear spiritual warfare. Let us take comfort in our faith
that You have already prevailed against the adversary.*

NATURAL RHYTHM

*"Come to me. Get away with me and you'll recover your
life. I'll show you how to take a real rest. Walk with
me and work with me—watch how I do it.
Learn the unforced rhythms of grace."*
MATTHEW 11:28–30 MSG

Take a moment right now to get away with Jesus. In His presence, you can find, get back, your true life—your life in and with Him. Only He can show you how to take a real break, one that includes His peace, His love, His strength, His nurturing. He is longing for you to take His hand, walk with Him, work with Him, play with Him. Jesus has set you an example, showing you how to spend more time with Father God. How to go up to the mountain alone and pray.

Learn the natural rhythm of God's good grace. He is waiting to show you. Are you willing to learn from Him and turn from the stress that dogs your steps?

*Lord, I'm willing to learn Your rhythm.
Help me recover my life!*

IN STEP WITH GOD

*It is the Lord Who goes before you; He will [march]
with you; He will not fail you or let you go or forsake
you; [let there be no cowardice or flinching, but] fear
not, neither become broken [in spirit—depressed,
dismayed, and unnerved with alarm].*
Deuteronomy 31:8 ampc

Moses was saying farewell to God's people, who would be led
into the Promised Land by Joshua. He told them God *Himself*
would go before them and give them victory. He encouraged
them by saying, "Be strong, courageous, and firm; fear not nor
be in terror before them, for it is the Lord your God Who goes
with you" (Deuteronomy 31:6 ampc).

As God went before His Israelites, He goes before you. He
marches with you as you enter His land of promises. Your role
is to not worry or fear but to believe God will neither fail nor
forsake you. When you trust God with all, keeping in step with
Him, you will prevail.

*I'm trusting in You, Lord, as we walk in step
together. Lead me to the land of Your promise.*

FEAR OF FEAR ITSELF

The fear of man brings a snare, but whoever
trusts in the LORD shall be safe.
PROVERBS 29:25 NKJV

Franklin D. Roosevelt stated these memorable words in his 1933 inaugural speech: ". . .the only thing we have to fear is fear itself." Four months later, panicked citizens pulled their money out of banks. Mass hysteria arose from their fear of fear itself.

The men who helped Caleb and Joshua check out the Promised Land said they felt like grasshoppers in the midst of giants. Their fear blinded them to the greatness of God.

Phobophobia is the fear of a phobia. A panic attack develops at the thought of coming across the feared phobia. My dread of downtown soured my stomach before I got in the car. But urgent business demanded my attention. I prayed for God to diminish my fear of the phobia of traffic, one-way streets, and limited parking. He answered as I paid the meter and walked two blocks to the county building.

Father God, help us remember that we can overcome
the unreasonable, unjustified terror that paralyzes
us only by placing our trust in You.

"NEVERTHELESS..."

The Jebusites, the inhabitants of the land. . .said to
David, "You will not come in here, but the blind and the
lame will ward you off"—thinking, "David cannot come
in here." Nevertheless, David took the stronghold of Zion.
2 SAMUEL 5:6–7 ESV

When you have God on your side, there is no need to stress and strain, even when people tell you your efforts will be useless. For God always has a "nevertheless" up His sleeve. His power can work through you when you stay in tune with His Spirit, allowing Him to rule your heart, mind, body, and soul. He will enable you to do above and beyond what you and others think you can do.

Let God's "nevertheless" ease your mind and strengthen your spirit. Know that God will build upon that which you accomplish in His power because, as He was with David, "the God of hosts" (2 Samuel 5:10 ESV) is with you.

Lord, help me see Your "nevertheless" in
all the challenges I face and know
that Your power is with me.

GOD HAS A PLAN

*"I know what I'm doing. I have it all planned out—
plans to take care of you, not abandon you, plans to
give you the future you hope for. When you call on me,
when you come and pray to me, I'll listen."*
JEREMIAH 29:11–12 MSG

Have you ever tried a new recipe and gotten flustered because you didn't know what you were doing? You're worried it won't end up looking just like the picture or tasting like it should?

Some new challenges in life can be like that. No matter how much you plan or how much effort you put into some new task, job, or project, you worry things will somehow go wrong and you may not be able to fix them!

Fortunately, God knows what *He's* doing—and He's infallible, so you need not worry about anything. God has everything planned out for you. He's going to take care of you, "to give you the future you hope for." So no worries. Just go to God in prayer. He's ready to listen.

*I'm thankful that You know what
You're doing, Lord. I'm counting on You!*

Day 205
FEAR OF HEIGHTS

Is not God in the height of heaven? and behold
the height of the stars, how high they are!
JOB 22:12 KJV

Fear of heights, like most immobilizing phobias, is partially rooted in not having control of our environment. The higher the elevation, the denser the breathable air. A loss of balance causes vertigo.

Another part of this fear might be from our quest to reach God. Climb the tallest tree; the heavens are higher. Take the elevator to the top of the Willis Tower in Chicago; the heavens are higher. Scale the jagged cliffs of Mount Everest; the heavens are higher. Soar toward the moon in a NASA rocket; the heavens are higher.

No matter how far above the ground we get, the heavens will always be above us. We can't reach God through our own works. In His great love for us, He came down as Jesus of Nazareth, to dwell with and suffer for His creation.

Heavenly Father, calm our fears of the
high places. Let us feel Your embrace
in our lowly place here on earth.

AT THE CENTER

*Let petitions and praises shape your worries into
prayers, letting God know your concerns. Before you
know it, a sense of God's wholeness, everything coming
together for good, will come and settle you down.
It's wonderful what happens when Christ displaces
worry at the center of your life.*
PHILIPPIANS 4:6–7 MSG

When worry overtakes you and stress rears its ugly head, stop
and do a self-check. What's at the center of your life? Who are
you sharing your concerns with? How are you sharing them?

If money, possessions, or people are at the center of your
life, you're bound to stray off course. If you're telling others all
your worries by ranting and raving, those worries become more
powerful, almost taking on a life of their own.

God wants you to come to Him with everything—no
matter how trivial you might think it is. As you pray, pepper
your petitions with praises. Doing so will not only change your
perspective but also give you a sense of God's peace as Christ
"displaces worry at the center of your life."

Let's talk, Lord. Be my center!

THE ART OF LIFE

*The steps of a [good] man are directed and established
by the Lord when He delights in his way [and He busies
Himself with his every step]. Though he falls, he shall
not be utterly cast down, for the Lord grasps his
hand in support and upholds him.*

PSALM 37:23–24 AMPC

Can you imagine exchanging worry for wonder? It's possible.
Journalist Malcom Muggeridge wrote, "Every happening, great
and small, is a parable whereby God speaks to us, and the art
of life is to get the message."

Instead of focusing on what may or may not happen or how
to fix the past, why not wonder what God may be saying to you
in the present? Come out of yourself and into God, looking
for His message through His Word, for the connection among
you, Him, and your life events. See where God's directing you,
where He's taking you.

Delight with wonder in every step along the way, knowing
that with your hand in Father God's, although you may stumble,
He'll never let you fall.

*Lord, help me discover Your message as I
delight in every step along the way.*

FEAR OF PANDEMIC DISEASES

*"Or if I should send a plague against that country
and pour out My wrath in blood on it."*
EZEKIEL 14:19 NASB

No disease existed in God's perfect world. But Adam's sin perverted the healthy environment God created. Since then, new diseases have emerged with deadly consequences.

The Black Death mushroomed from China to India to Persia to Syria and to Egypt. Twenty million Europeans died after trade ships brought it to Italy. People back then believed God delivered this plague as punishment for their sin. Did they know the Lord's warning in Ezekiel of a plague against His people for their idolatrous sin? Perhaps they remembered the Angel of Death passing over those who had the lamb's blood on their doorposts.

The deadliest plague we face today is the spread of agnosticism. While biological diseases might take lives, the sin of unbelief can take souls. The Word of God is the only healer.

*Almighty God, help us to put the blood of the Lamb
on the doorposts of our hearts to protect us
while we spread the Gospel of Jesus
Christ throughout the world.*

AMAZING EXCHANGE

*In peace I will both lie down and sleep, for You, Lord,
alone make me dwell in safety and confident trust.*
PSALM 4:8 AMPC

When we pray before our head hits the pillow—with all our
heart, body, mind, soul, and strength—laying all our worries
and stressors at God's feet, an amazing exchange takes place.
Jesus takes all our problems upon His shoulders and gives us
His peace. As we put ourselves in His embrace, He surrounds
us with His protection. We are little sheep in the arms of the
Great Shepherd, the One who promises to lead us beside still
waters and take us to green pastures.

In this way only can we lie down and sleep in peace. For
only in His arms, His presence, His light are we truly safe,
trusting that as He is with us in the dark night, He will yet be
with us in the morning light.

*I pray then place myself in Your loving care, Lord.
Watch me through the night.*

PERFECT LOVE

And as we live in God, our love grows more perfect.
So we will not be afraid. . . . Such love has no fear.
1 John 4:17–18 NLT

As you purpose to live in God's love, you're not only living in Him, but He's living in you! Communing with Him, there's no room for anything else—no worries, no fears, no anger, no doubts. God loves you so much that He'll never let anything come between you and Him. Nor will He let anything or anyone snatch you out of His hand.

Today, pray that God will help you open your heart to the power and peace of His love, that your spirit and His will meld into one. Then spend some time in God's presence, allowing His love to pour into you, feed and nourish you, and fill you until it spills out of you and onto those around you.

Lord, I want that perfect love I get only when I am
living in Your love and You're living in me.
Fill me, Lord, with such love.

COURAGE IN THE FACE OF DEATH

*We are of good courage, I say, and prefer rather to be
absent from the body and to be at home with the Lord.*
2 CORINTHIANS 5:8 NASB

How do we stare down an enemy as menacing as death?

Although God created us to live forever, death entered the
garden when the Lord had to kill an animal to cover the sins
of Adam and Eve. They were then evicted, lest they eat of the
tree of life. He loves us too much to let us live eternally with
the stain of rebellion separating us from His grace.

I've stared down that old enemy in the loss of my parents,
relatives, close friends, and my beloved husband. Each time, I
took comfort in the Lord's loving embrace and the knowledge
that, because they believed in Jesus Christ, they prefer to be
absent from the body and present with the Lord.

*Gracious God, thank You for giving Your Son, Jesus,
to vanquish the last enemy on the cross. We who
believe in Him won't be separated from Your
love when we leave this earth.*

THOUGHTS

"For my thoughts are not your thoughts,
neither are your ways my ways, declares the Lord.
For as the heavens are higher than the earth,
so are my ways higher than your ways and
my thoughts than your thoughts."
Isaiah 55:8–9 esv

Every minute of the day we have thoughts going through our minds, whether or not we're conscious of them. But if we'd stop in our meanderings and zero in on what we are telling ourselves (or others), we might find some of our thoughts are causing us (or others) stress.

God's thoughts aren't our thoughts. He makes that perfectly clear. But we can change our thoughts to be more like His. We can renew our minds every morning and throughout the day to be more like His. We can sing ourselves a new song, one filled with His promises instead of our problems, His encouragement instead of our discouragement. Make your thoughts more like God's and you'll transform your world.

Lord, help me become more aware of my thoughts.
Help me change them up to match
Your way of thinking.

Day 213

BECOMING UNSINKABLE

Jesus immediately reached out his hand and took hold of him, saying to him, "O you of little faith, why did you doubt?"
MATTHEW 14:31 ESV

After telling His followers to take the boat to the other side of the lake, Jesus went up on a mountain to pray. When darkness set in, the boat was still far from the shore, caught in a storm.

So Jesus came to them, walking on the water. When the disciples saw Him, they cried out in fear. But Jesus immediately told them, "Take heart; it is I. Do not be afraid" (Matthew 14:27 ESV). That's when Peter got brave, saying, "If it's You, Jesus, tell me to come to You." Jesus did, prompting Peter to get out of the boat and begin walking on the water. But then he saw the wind, got scared, and began sinking, crying out to Jesus, "Save me!" And Jesus did! (See Matthew 14:28-31.)

The point? If you keep your eyes on Jesus, focusing on Him rather than your circumstances, Jesus will enable you to do things you never dreamed possible!

With You, Jesus, I'm unsinkable!
Tell me to come to You!

Day 214
SINKING STRESS

"Embrace this God-life. . .and nothing will be too much for you. This mountain, for instance: Just say, 'Go jump in the lake'—no shuffling or hemming and hawing— and it's as good as done. That's why I urge you to pray for absolutely everything."
MARK 11:23–24 MSG

Everyday stressors can turn into mountainous obstacles if we let them. But Jesus has provided a way out for us. He tells us to pray for "absolutely everything" and to put our belief in Him behind our prayers. When we do, when we fully "embrace this God-life," we will find that anything and everything is possible.

So put your wholehearted belief behind God's promises. Claim that nothing is impossible to you who believes (see Mark 9:23). That with God, no one and nothing can stand against you (see Romans 8:31). Speak God's promises to the mountain of stress in front of you. Doing so will pry it loose, lift it up, and toss it into the sea.

I'm wholeheartedly embracing this God-life, Lord! I'm claiming Your promises and watching my stress sink into the sea.

A NEW SONG

Sing GOD a brand-new song! Earth and everyone in it,
sing! Sing to GOD—worship GOD!
PSALM 96:1 MSG

What song was in your head this morning? What might you have been mindlessly humming this afternoon? What might be "playing" in your head this evening? What chorus might you hear when your head hits the pillow?

Homing in on what we're humming and changing up the song can transform our lives. And when we change up that song in our heads to echo one of God's promises or truths, we are, in effect, worshipping our great God.

The most effective way of doing this is to claim each thought. What is it telling you? Does it agree with God's promises or truths? If not, replace it with what God would have you think. In effect, you'll be using God's amazing Word to overpower what the deceiver may have planted in your brain. Here's a general song to help you begin disarming the lies that lead to stress:

The Lord is my Shepherd [to feed, guide, and shield
me], I shall not lack (Psalm 23:1 AMPC).

CHOOSE JOY

*"He shall eat curds and honey when he knows
how to refuse the evil and choose the good."*
ISAIAH 7:15 ESV

Every day you have the freedom to make choices. To choose good over evil, right over wrong, God's Way over your way, and joy over worry. That's a lot of choices, each one having its own set of repercussions. The choosing good over evil, right over wrong, and God's Way over your own seems self-explanatory. You ask God what to do and you do it.

But how do you choose joy over worry? It's simple: You open your eyes to the blessings around you.

Author Marianne Williamson wrote, "Joy is what happens when we allow ourselves to recognize how good things really are." Today—and every day—choose to do just that. Write a list of things that are going right in your life. Then thank God for all He has done for you, and your joy will blossom.

> *Help me, Lord, to choose joy, to recognize all the
> good in my life, other people, and this world.*

Day 217

GOD-PERSPECTIVE

*They brought the Israelites an evil report of
the land which they had scouted out, saying,
The land through which we went to spy it out
is a land that devours its inhabitants.*

NUMBERS 13:32 AMPC

Out of the twelve scouts Moses sent into the Promised Land, ten came back with an "evil report," saying, "There we saw the Nephilim. . .who come from the giants; and we were in our own sight as grasshoppers, and so we were in their sight" (Numbers 13:33 AMPC). Yet Caleb told the people, "Let us go up at once and possess it; we are well able to conquer it" (Numbers 13:30 AMPC).

The first report was evil because those ten scouts had imagined the challenges before them as being bigger than their God! But Caleb, imagining God beside him, knew nothing could defeat them. Because of Caleb's God-perspective, the Lord said, "He has a different spirit; he follows me passionately. I'll bring him into the land that he scouted and his children will inherit it" (Numbers 14:24 MSG).

*Help me, Lord, to see You standing beside
me in every challenge I face.*

ZEROING IN

*And Jesus said to him, What do you
want Me to do for you?*
MARK 10:51 AMPC

Stress can come upon us when we find ourselves running after a million different things, unable (or unwilling) to zero in on exactly what we want. When Jesus encountered a blind beggar calling out His name, He stopped and asked him, "What do you want Me to do for you?" Although Jesus knew the man wanted sight, not alms, He made no move until the beggar said to Him: "Master, let me receive my sight" (Mark 10:51 AMPC). "And Jesus said to him, Go your way; your faith has healed you. And at once he received his sight and accompanied Jesus on the road" (Mark 10:52 AMPC).

Take some time now to stop and consider: What do you really want Jesus to do for you? Then pray and go your way, and your faith will heal you as you follow Jesus down the road.

*Lord, help me to zero in on what I really want then
trust in You as I follow Your pathway.*

Day 219
RADIANT WITH HOPE

*May the God of hope fill you with joy and peace in your
faith, that by the power of the Holy Spirit, your whole
life and outlook may be radiant with hope.*
ROMANS 15:13 PHILLIPS

Tired of letting your worries fill your mind, guiding your
decisions and keeping you from living the life God wants you
to live? Why not fill your mind with God before worry has a
chance to rear its ugly head?

Artist Howard Chandler Christy had a good method you
might want to follow. He said, "Every morning I spend fifteen
minutes filling my mind full of God; and so there's no room
left for worry thoughts." Sounds like a plan!

This morning, before your mind has a chance to run away
with itself, fill it full of God. Begin with a short, "Good morning, Glory!" prayer. Then read a portion of the Bible, looking
for a message from the Author of your faith. Finally, pray as
the Spirit leads, allowing Him to give you His outlook, radiant
with hope!

Good morning, Glory! Fill my mind! Give me hope!

SPINNING OUR WHEELS

*I have strength for all things in Christ Who empowers
me [I am ready for anything and equal to anything
through Him Who infuses inner strength into me;
I am self-sufficient in Christ's sufficiency].*

<small>PHILIPPIANS 4:13 AMPC</small>

Oftentimes stress comes to us because we think we are strong
enough to do it all, regardless of what our spiritual life and
practice look like. But Jesus has clearly told us that unless we
have a close and active relationship with Him, abiding in Him
24–7, we'll only be spinning our wheels. Because apart from
Him, we can do nothing (see John 15:5).

Thus, we need to delve daily into the Word, believe God's
promises, walk in His Way, and pray, pray, pray. When we do,
we realize we don't need to do it all. But for what He wants us
to do, He'll give us all the strength we need.

*I know I am nothing without You, Lord.
So I come to You now for the strength to
do what You have called me to do.*

THE REMEDY OF FORGIVENESS

*Clothe yourselves with tenderhearted mercy,
kindness, humility, gentleness, and patience.
Make allowance for each other's faults, and forgive
anyone who offends you. Remember, the Lord
forgave you, so you must forgive others.*

COLOSSIANS 3:12–13 NLT

It's amazing how well God knows His people, how much His Word is a remedy for all our ills. God knows forgiveness benefits us not only spiritually but physically as well. In fact, forgiving others has been proven to lower not only stress but depression—and blood pressure! It also improves cholesterol levels and sleep! But it's not just saying the words "I forgive you"; it's making a conscious decision to release all your negative feelings toward that person and what he or she has done—whether or not you believe the individual deserves your forgiveness. Even if that person is yourself.

And the bonus to all this is that as you forgive others, God forgives you! So go deep. Check in with yourself. Who do you need to forgive?

*Lord, bring to my mind those I need to forgive,
and help me to do so in this moment.*

EVERY MOMENT BECOMES A PRAYER

Seek God while he's here to be found,
pray to him while he's close at hand.
ISAIAH 55:6 MSG

God wants you to seek Him, to pray to Him while He's near. But as you're striving to meet project deadlines, get your chores done, pick up the kids, volunteer at church, and so much more, prayer seems to fall by the wayside. You begin worrying God sees you as a slacker. How can you pray without ceasing when you barely have time to fit in a shower?

God didn't devise prayer to be just one more to-do. So perhaps it's time to change your perspective of prayer.

Frank Bianco, a journalist and photographer, wrote, "If you begin to live life looking for the God that is all around you, every moment becomes a prayer." Try doing that today, seeing God in everything that surrounds you and lifting up your thanks as you live in God's wonderland.

Reveal Yourself to me, Lord,
in all I do and see. Make every
moment of my life a prayer to You.

GOD'S GOODNESS

*[What, what would have become of me] had I
not believed that I would see the Lord's goodness
in the land of the living! Wait and hope for and
expect the Lord; be brave and of good courage
and let your heart be stout and enduring.*

PSALM 27:13–14 AMPC

When we feel as if the world is crashing down upon us, it can be difficult, if not impossible, to lift ourselves up. That's when we need to muster all the energy we have to ponder the words of Psalm 27:13–14 and then write them upon our hearts. For only God and His Word have the power to lift us up out of ourselves and into His light.

King David of the Bible, the author of these verses, knew that to keep his head above the fray, he had to have faith, to believe he would see God bring something good into his life—no matter how dire the situation. With courage and perseverance, he then waited in expectation of God's goodness.

*I know I'll see Your goodness in
this land and in my life, Lord!*

TRUST

*Trust (lean on, rely on, and be confident)
in the Lord and do good; so shall you dwell in
the land and feed surely on His faithfulness,
and truly you shall be fed.*
PSALM 37:3 AMPC

God wants you to trust in Him. To actually lean on Him, knowing He alone can hold you up, give you the strength to stand. He wants you to know you can rely on Him, confident that what He has promised in His Word is a promise to you personally, no holds barred. When you have that trust, you can then do as He wishes. You can lead a life of stressing less, of following in His steps, of doing His good. And when you are leading that kind of life, believing in Him with your entire heart, all your needs will be provided for.

Trust in God, the One who has loved you and provided for you from the beginning, and all else will fall into place.

*Lord, I am counting on You, trusting You are
holding me in Your hand. Help me to
rest secure in that knowledge.*

A GOOD MEASURE

"Give, and it will be given to you. Good measure, pressed down, shaken together, running over, will be put into your lap. For with the measure you use it will be measured back to you."

LUKE 6:38 ESV

Jesus wants you to treat others well, for when you bless them, God will bless you back. Yet it may be difficult to give of yourself or your resources when you're worried you won't "have enough" for yourself.

It's time to change up that mindset. Let your worries of lack fall by the wayside and start making this world a better place by giving to others, whether by serving in church, volunteering at a food bank, donating to a charity, helping a neighbor plant a garden, or giving a blanket to a homeless shelter.

Begin by doing one little thing for someone you know or even a complete stranger. Write down what you've done, including how you were rewarded in return, and soon your worries around lack will be a dim memory.

Show me what I can do today, Jesus,
to bless the life of another.

TRUE DELIGHT

*Delight yourself also in the Lord, and He will give
you the desires and secret petitions of your heart.*
PSALM 37:4 AMPC

It's easy to get stressed out, pulled in a thousand different ways
as we try to fulfill our own desires or those of other people.
In the quest to "satisfy" ourselves or others, our true path is
obscured. Then when we actually obtain what we (or others)
desire, we find that either it doesn't satisfy or another desire is
just around the corner, and we begin the chase all over again.

God wants you to realize the only desire that can give you
true rest and peace in this life is delighting yourself in Him,
making closeness and fellowship with Him your only goal. Doing
so not only will put all your other desires in their rightful place
as your wants begin to line up with His, but it will give you rest
from chasing the seemingly never-ending wants.

*Lord, I'm setting myself down, giving myself time
to just rest and take pleasure in You—
my true delight and desire.*

BRINGING OUT THE BEST

Commit your way to the Lord [roll and repose each care of your load on Him]; trust (lean on, rely on, and be confident) also in Him and He will bring it to pass.

PSALM 37:5 AMPC

Turn everything in Your life over to God and trust that He will give you all the strength, wisdom, and help you need as you walk with Him. Let all the insults, problems, issues, comments, stresses roll right off your back and into His hands. He'll know what to do with them. Rest in the knowledge that you can trust God; He knows what He is doing, He sees the end, and all things will work out for good.

Have confidence in the One who was trusted by Abraham, whose son was saved by a ram. Rely on the One who was trusted by Joseph, a slave, then a prisoner, and finally a powerful ruler in Egypt.

Lord, I'm committing my way to You,
knowing You will bring out the best in me.

Day 228

BEAMING WITH LOVE

*Neither death nor life, neither messenger of Heaven
nor monarch of earth, neither what happens today
nor what may happen tomorrow, neither a power
from on high nor a power from below, nor anything
else in God's whole world has any power to separate
us from the love of God in Jesus Christ our Lord!*
ROMANS 8:38–39 PHILLIPS

People may come against you. They may even walk out of your life or stop loving you. But you need not worry that you will ever be separated from God's love, for His love is unconditional. No matter what happens, He will love you. His love is an unbreakable cord between you and Him.

Pray that God will open your heart to His love. That you will feel that joyful love beaming down into you, surrounding you, cushioning you, holding you, blessing you, warming you, feeding you every moment of this day, giving you the confidence to walk His way regardless of what others do and say.

*Abba God, beam Your love into
my heart as I rest in You.*

QUIETNESS AND CONTENTMENT

Be still and rest in the Lord; wait for Him and patiently lean yourself upon Him; fret not yourself because of him who prospers in his way.

PSALM 37:7 AMPC

As you begin to alleviate your stress by trusting and delighting yourself in the Lord, committing your way to Him, you will find yourself more still, more at peace, more able to rest in God. You will stop comparing your life to the lives of others who always seem to be one step ahead of you. Instead, you'll be patiently waiting for God, expecting and knowing He will do all good things in His time. You need not fear or fret. You and your life are in God's good hands, and this knowledge brings a wonderful new quiet and contentment into your life, a steadiness you've never experienced before.

Lord, here I am, leaning back upon You,
listening to Your breath as it aligns with mine.
Fill me with peace beyond understanding as I
commit my path and desires to You, trusting
and delighting in You and Your love.

DO WHAT YOU CAN

"She did what she could when she could."
MARK 14:8 MSG

In Mark 14, a woman, her heart and spirit prompted by God, poured expensive perfume on Jesus' head. Witnesses muttered that she wasted perfume that could have been sold and the money given to the poor. But Jesus told them to leave her alone: "She did what she could when she could—she pre-anointed my body for burial. And you can be sure. . .what she just did is going to be talked about admiringly" (verses 8–9 MSG).

God wants you to be open to the Spirit and follow His promptings, to do what He would have you do, with what He gives you, when you can do it. And put the results, comments, consequences in His hands. Each day, listen, do, let what you didn't get done go, and then rest in Him, satisfied you have done what you could.

Lord, help me to do what I can and leave the rest in Your amazingly capable hands.

THE WOMAN WHO STICKS WITH GOD

*"Blessed is the man who trusts me, GOD, the woman
who sticks with GOD. They're like trees. . .putting down
roots near the rivers—never a worry through the
hottest of summers, never dropping a leaf,
serene and calm through droughts."*
JEREMIAH 17:7–8 MSG

Not only does worry sap your strength and energy, it also keeps you from creating, from being productive. God knows this only too well. That's why He tells you that you're blessed when you trust in Him and stick with Him and His plan. When you believe His promises.

When you trust in God, He says you're like a tree whose roots have access to His river of life. Even through the hottest drought, you'll still be fresh. By being confident in Him, calm and serene, you'll be "bearing fresh fruit every season" (Jeremiah 17:8 MSG).

Trust God. And you'll be blessed in all things, at all times, and in all ways.

*I'm sticking with You, Lord, refusing to let
winds of worry have any sway over me.*

FIRST A RESPONDER

When I am afraid, I put my trust in you. In God, whose word I praise, in God I trust; I shall not be afraid. . . . This I know, that God is for me. In God, whose word I praise, in the LORD, whose word I praise, in God I trust; I shall not be afraid.

PSALM 56:3–4, 9–11 ESV

David wrote the above words when he was in trouble. Three times he talks of his trust in God, how because of that trust, he need not fear anything or anyone. Three times he says he praises God's Word, reminding himself of how God's promises have come true for him in the past. And amid all this trusting and praising, he writes eight power-filled words: "This I know, that God is for me."

Use these words to help you be a responder instead of a reactor when stressful situations arise.

I need not fear because I know You are for me, God.
I praise You and the power of Your Word!

AWAKE REJOICING

This is the day that the LORD has made;
let us rejoice and be glad in it.
PSALM 118:24 ESV

Dale Evans Rogers said, "Every day we live is a priceless gift of God, loaded with possibilities to learn something new, to gain fresh insights." How wonder-filled would our day be if we awoke rejoicing because of the new day the Lord has made for us?

Why not deter stress by memorizing the words of Psalm 118:24 and saying them aloud before your feet hit the floor each day? Be curious about what you might learn that day, what God-incidence (i.e., a spiritual coincidence) might occur. Keep your eyes open for God's hand in all circumstances. And praise Him for the beauty of the ordinary, everyday people and things that surround you. Let your joy transform your face into a smile as you experience the priceless gift of life.

I'm rejoicing in the precious moments You have given
me today, Lord, and keeping my eyes open for You!

YOUR BEST DEFENSE

*"Don't be afraid! Stand still, and see what the L*ORD *will do to save you today. You will never see these Egyptians again. The L*ORD *is fighting for you! So be still!"*
EXODUS 14:13–14 GW

God had taken His people out of their comfort zone, and their worry grew to panic. They began thinking it would be better if they were slaves back in Egypt instead of between the Egyptian army and the Red Sea. But Moses told them not to worry or be afraid, to merely stand still and watch what God was going to do. They'd never see these warriors again because God was fighting for them.

And God won the day! He parted the sea for His people and brought the waters back to drown the attackers.

You're God's daughter, one of His people. He'll defend you no matter what. Your job is not to worry or panic but to stand still and watch Him work!

You, Lord, are my best and most powerful defense. As for me, I'm going to simply stand still and watch You win the day!

THE TOWER OF POWER

The name of the Lord is a strong tower;
the [consistently] righteous man [upright
and in right standing with God] runs into
it and is safe, high [above evil] and strong.
PROVERBS 18:10 AMPC

Some days there is nowhere to go but up. It's a fact. Not all moments in our day are going to be rosy. But thankfully God has provided an exit plan for just such harrowing, stress-filled moments. When the going gets tough, get going to God. Shout His name and head for His presence. Run, climb, escape to Him—mentally, spiritually, emotionally, even physically if a church or chapel is nearby—a place of safety and strength, high above anything you are going through. With His presence surrounding you, nothing can really harm you. And you are given a space to catch your breath, calm your spirit, quiet your mind, settle your soul. Stay as long as you'd like until you're ready to face the challenge before you.

I'm running to You, Lord, my tower of power.
For in You, I know I'm safe.

WEIGHED DOWN

Cast your burden on the Lord [releasing the weight of it] and He will sustain you; He will never allow the [consistently] righteous to be moved (made to slip, fall, or fail).

PSALM 55:22 AMPC

Proverbs 12:25 says, "Anxiety in a man's heart weighs it down" (AMPC). So what are we to do with our worries and stresses that have become so burdensome we are stooped low and feel we can no longer breathe? God wants us to come to Him every day—or every moment of every day, if needed—and leave all that weight on our hearts in His hands. When we do, He may not remove us from whatever situation we find ourselves in, but He'll keep us strong and give us peace in the midst of it. And once our hearts, minds, and souls are no longer burdened, God will make sure no one and nothing will push us off the course He's set for our lives.

What anxiety is weighing you down? Give it to God; then stand tall.

Lord, show me what burdens I need to give You.

TRUST IN THE LORD

Don't worry about the wicked or envy those who do wrong. For like grass, they soon fade away. Like spring flowers, they soon wither. Trust in the LORD and do good. Then you will live safely in the land and prosper.

PSALM 37:1–3 NLT

Sometimes it seems those who get all the breaks are the people who don't believe in God. In fact, the more they lie and cheat, going against all rules and laws, the more they seem to prosper! Yet here you are, doing the right thing, at least most of the time, and you can't seem to get ahead.

God tells you not to worry about those who are walking down the dark path. It's *you* who's truly prospering. While you're on the road to eternal life, storing up treasures in heaven, the ne'er-do-wells will quickly fade away, unable to take their gains with them.

So take heart. Trust in God, leaving everything and everyone in His hands. He'll make things come out right.

Lord, help me keep my eyes on You and what You'd have me do—for in You I truly prosper!

OUT OF THE DEPTHS

The God of heaven. . .gives wisdom to the wise and knowledge to those who have understanding! He reveals the deep and secret things; He knows what is in the darkness, and the light dwells with Him!

DANIEL 2:19, 21–22 AMPC

When you don't know what to do, when you are searching for an answer, when you are stressing for a blessing, go to God's Word. See it as "the Word of God which speaks out of the depths of an almost unimaginable past into the depths of ourselves" (Frederick Buechner, *Listening to Your Life*, June 14 reading).

Within God's story lies your own. Pray that He will give you the wisdom and knowledge you need to rise above your distress. Look for the secret He is aching to impart. Let Him show you the path to His light. Determine to allow His deep to call to your deep (see Psalm 42:7).

God, speak out of Your depths and into mine. Reveal in Your Word what You would have me know.

GOD'S DRAW

In my distress I cried out to the LORD; yes,
I prayed to my God for help. He heard me
from his sanctuary; my cry to him reached his
ears. . . . He reached down from heaven and
rescued me; he drew me out of deep waters.
PSALM 18:6, 16 NLT

In times when you don't know what to do, where to go, turn to God in prayer. Imagine God's right hand reaching out to save you. Know that He will give you whatever strength and encouragement you need to continue on. He will protect you from all that's coming against you.

Never doubt that God has a plan for your life and is working it out—even this very moment. You opened this book to this page and are reading these words for a reason. For reassurance that God is still speaking into your life with a love beyond comprehension.

Lord, I rest in the knowledge that You will
see me through all things, that You will
give me the strength I need to live the
life You've planned for me.

COMMIT YOUR WAY TO GOD

*Commit your way to the Lord [roll and repose each
care of your load on Him]; trust (lean on, rely on,
and be confident) also in Him and He will bring
it to pass. And He will make your uprightness and
right standing with God go forth as the light.*
PSALM 37:5–6 AMPC

Wondering about where to go, what to do? Worried you might have taken a wrong turn somewhere? Relax. Let God know all of your concerns. Allow them to roll off your back and onto His. Trust that the Master Planner will show you the way you're to go.

God hasn't left you alone. He, His Son Jesus, and the Holy Spirit are here to watch over and look out for you. They know the past, present, and future, hold all wisdom, and wield supernatural power. They see what you're doing, where you're going, what you're thinking, and where your heart is. Open yourself to them, be responsive to their prompts, and you will never lose your way.

Show me the way, Lord, as I shine for You!

ARMS WIDE OPEN

*Carefully build yourselves up in this most holy faith by
praying in the Holy Spirit, staying right at the center of
God's love, keeping your arms open and outstretched,
ready for the mercy of our Master, Jesus Christ.
This is the unending life, the real life!*
JUDE 1:20–21 MSG

Sometimes a woman prays an SOS prayer: "God, help me!"
Sometimes she prays out of habit, using words so rehearsed or
so-long memorized that their meaning is obscured, unrealized,
forgotten. Then there are prayers that are based not on God's
will but on her own agenda, wants, desires, needs.

To build up her faith, a woman is advised to pray in the
Holy Spirit. That means praying in rhythm with the Spirit, in
agreement with His will. That's how she will stay at the center
of God's love with arms wide open, ready to receive all Jesus
has to offer.

*Help me, Holy Spirit, to be in harmony with
Your will, Your agenda, Your plans, not mine.
Keep me at the center of God's love.*

CALLING GOD

*"This is God's Message, the God who made earth,
made it livable and lasting, known everywhere
as God: 'Call to me and I will answer you. I'll tell
you marvelous and wondrous things that you
could never figure out on your own.' "*
JEREMIAH 33:3 MSG

You never know when God is going to reveal something to you, some truth you need to know, some secret to help you connect the dots, see His hand, discover the solution, find some hope. And God can deliver that message no matter where you are! (Jeremiah received the words of 33:3 while he was locked up in jail!) But you have to call on God. You have to pray to Him. When you do, He'll answer you, telling you things you otherwise would never know! He—the Creator of the universe, the One who knows how everything works—will help you figure things out.

The formula is simple: Call. Pray. Listen. Then marvel at the wonder of the knowledge of God.

*Dear Lord, here I am! Speak!
Tell me what You'd have me know.*

GOOD TALKS

Let no corrupting talk come out of your mouths, but
only such as is good for building up, as fits the occasion,
that it may give grace to those who hear.
Ephesians 4:29 esv

Your words have power, affecting those around you. That's why you must be careful not to pollute another person's thoughts with your worries. By voicing them, you may cause others to take on your worries as their own, and you may end up reinforcing your concerns in your own mind. Before you know it, your proposed what-ifs have become contagious, full-blown fears!

Instead of voicing worries, consider saying uplifting things to yourself and others, such as, "We can do all things with Christ's strength" (see Philippians 4:13). Or, "God will make a way" (see 1 Corinthians 10:13). Or, "I believe I'll see the goodness of the Lord in this world" (see Psalm 27:13). Whatever fits the occasion.

In saying good things, you'll be building up the faith of others as well as your own!

Lord, help me speak words of Your wisdom instead of
voicing my worries. Make me a builder not a wrecker.

Day 244
GET GOING

GOD addressed Samuel: "So, how long are you going to mope over Saul? You know I've rejected him as king over Israel. Fill your flask with anointing oil and get going. I'm sending you to Jesse of Bethlehem. I've spotted the very king I want among his sons."
1 SAMUEL 16:1 MSG

You had a plan. But things didn't turn out the way you thought they would. Yet you still seem to be sulking, brooding over what seems to be a lost opportunity, mourning what could've been, maybe even trying to force things to work out right.

God wants you to stop stressing over what could've been. He's ready for you to move on, to get going, to take the next step in His plan.

Ask God what His next move for you is. He has already spotted your next opportunity to cooperate with His plan and work out His good for all concerned. So what are you waiting for? Get going.

I'm not sure, Lord, why things didn't work out, but I know You have a plan. So I'm ready, Lord. Where to?

GOD IN ACTION

"When two of you get together on anything at all on earth and make a prayer of it, my Father in heaven goes into action. And when two or three of you are together because of me, you can be sure that I'll be there."
MATTHEW 18:20 MSG

Author Emily Kimbrough said, "Remember, we all stumble, every one of us. That's why it's a comfort to go hand in hand." God takes this further in Ecclesiastes 4:12 by telling us, "By yourself you're unprotected. With a friend you can face the worst. Can you round up a third? A three-stranded rope isn't easily snapped" (MSG).

Jesus makes this idea even more powerful. He says when two pray, our Father God "goes into action"! And when believers are together in Jesus' name, we can be certain He's right in the thick of things!

So stress less by grabbing a believer (or two) by the hand. Tap into the comfort and strength a duo or threesome provides. Expect Jesus to join you. And watch God go into action!

Here we are, Lord! We're tapping into You!

A FAITH-FILLED WOMAN

*I am calling up memories of your sincere and
unqualified faith (the leaning of your entire personality
on God in Christ in absolute trust and confidence in
His power, wisdom, and goodness), [a faith] that first
lived permanently in [the heart of] your grandmother
Lois and your mother Eunice and now, I am [fully]
persuaded, [dwells] in you also.*

2 TIMOTHY 1:5 AMPC

How you live out your faith makes an impression on young minds. When your children and grandchildren or someone else's children look at your life, will they see you as a female fretter or a woman warrior?

The apostle Paul was Timothy's spiritual father. In his letter to the young man, Paul recalls Timothy's mother and grandmother, how their sincere faith was an example for Timothy to follow, paving the way for him to totally believe in Christ.

May you, like Timothy's mother and grandmother, become much more of a prayer warrior than a worrier, a peace- and faith-filled woman whom others can look to and emulate.

*Dear Lord, make me a prayerful woman,
full of peace and strong in faith.*

PATIENT FAITH

But God remembered Noah and all the beasts and all the
livestock that were with him in the ark. And God made a
wind blow over the earth, and the waters subsided.
Genesis 8:1 esv

Thinking that God has forgotten you? That He has left you adrift in a stress storm lasting forty days and nights? Don't believe those lies for a minute. God remembers you.

Just when you think the waters of chaos couldn't get any higher, God will stop the flood. As the waters begin to recede, He'll set you to rest on dry land. And as the waters continue to abate, God will renew the world around you, preparing the ground for your next step upon dry land.

Be patient. For Noah, 370 days passed between the first drop of rain and the moment Noah and company left the ark. Have faith. For it was by and because of faith that Noah followed God, built an ark, saved his family, and had the opportunity to become "intimate with God" (Hebrews 11:7 msg).

I'm trusting in Your timing, Lord.
Bless my faith.

CELEBRATING THE SPIRITUAL WOMAN

Therefore we do not become discouraged (utterly
spiritless, exhausted, and wearied out through fear).
Though our outer man is [progressively] decaying
and wasting away, yet our inner self is being
[progressively] renewed day after day.
2 CORINTHIANS 4:16 AMPC

Yes, our bodies are changing day by day. From the minute we are born, our earth suits begin to wear out. That's the not-so-good news. The better news is that no matter what's happening to our outer woman (physical self), the inner woman (spiritual self) is being refreshed, renewed, day after day! That's because "we consider and look not to the things that are seen but to the things that are unseen; for the things that are visible are temporal (brief and fleeting), but the things that are invisible are deathless and everlasting" (2 Corinthians 4:18 AMPC).

So, keeping your eyes on Christ, stop stressing over the new laugh lines, and instead celebrate the beauty of your inner spirit.

Lord, I don't want to be focused on the material girl
but rather celebrate the spiritual woman!
Help me keep my eyes on the unseen.

SOMETHING NEW

The Lord makes a path through the sea and a road
through the strong currents. . . . Forget what happened
in the past, and do not dwell on events from long ago.
I am going to do something new. It is already
happening. Don't you recognize it?
Isaiah 43:16, 18–19 gw

God is the only being powerful enough to actually make a path through the sea, a road through the riptide. But you'll never see that new path or road if you're spending your time today ruminating over what happened yesterday.

God wants you living in the present moment, expecting the unexpected. He's going to do something totally new in your life. In fact, He's already doing it! Do you see it? He's going to "clear a way in the desert," to "make rivers on dry land" (Isaiah 43:19 gw).

So put your worries about the past behind you. Keep your eyes open to where God's working! You'll be sure to see a new path ahead.

Lord, I'm ready to expect the unexpected!
My eyes are focused on the new road
You've already paved ahead!

TAKE CONFIDENCE

"With him is an arm of flesh, but with us is the LORD our God, to help us and to fight our battles." And the people took confidence from the words of Hezekiah king of Judah.

2 CHRONICLES 32:8 ESV

Much of stress comes from lack of confidence in our abilities, lack of faith that God can help us do all He's called us to do.

But the truth is that because God is in our lives, He's empowering and equipping us to do all He wants us to do—no matter how big or small the job! And God is not just an arm of flesh, a sometimes-there human helper. He's the Lord of the universe, the Master Planner, the One who can make the sun stop in the sky! Take confidence from those facts! Know that He's helping you fight every battle you encounter. As He does, others who see it will know that "this work [was] accomplished with the help of our God" (Nehemiah 6:16 ESV).

Grow my confidence in You, Lord!

OUT OF LINE

*If we live by the [Holy] Spirit, let us also walk
by the Spirit. [If by the Holy Spirit we have our
life in God, let us go forward walking in line,
our conduct controlled by the Spirit.]*

GALATIANS 5:25 AMPC

When stress begins to rule our lives, the root cause is apt to be that we are following the world instead of the Word, in step with society instead of the Spirit. Stress is a signal that we are to stop, look up from the path our feet are on, and take stock of where we are standing. Then we must choose to get back on track, back in line with what we profess as Christians, asking God to recalculate our route, to change the vision we have before us, from ours to His, before we stumble even further away from what He would have us be and do.

*Lord, I have stepped out of line with the Spirit.
Help me get back on His path. Show me the
way I should go. Change my thoughts
to be more like Yours.*

THE SPIRIT OF FREEDOM

Those who trust God's action in them find that
God's Spirit is in them—living and breathing God!
Obsession with self in these matters is a dead end;
attention to God leads us out into the open,
into a spacious, free life.
ROMANS 8:6–7 MSG

Worry is a reminder that every moment you have a choice as to
what kind of life you want to live—in the spirit or in the flesh. If
your mind is on the flesh, you become an enslaved worrier, but
if your mind is on God's Spirit, you become God's free warrior.

It comes down to where your focus is. The Message puts it
this way: "Focusing on the self is the opposite of focusing on
God. Anyone completely absorbed in self ignores God, ends up
thinking more about self than God. That person ignores who
God is and what he is doing" (Romans 8:8).

Today choose to trust in God and be a free woman warrior.

Lord, lead me out of myself and into You,
where I'll find the peace and freedom I crave.

EVERYTHING WE NEED

We're depending on GOD; he's everything we need.
What's more, our hearts brim with joy since we've taken
for our own his holy name. Love us, GOD, with all
you've got—that's what we're depending on.
PSALM 33:20–21 MSG

There's no reason to stress when we realize that God is everything we need. He is our help, our shield, our fortress. When we are abiding in Him, we are filled with the joy His presence brings.

Other humans will let us down. That's a given. But God won't. We can depend on Him through thick and thin. He constantly has His eye upon us, watching, waiting to step in and save us when we get stuck. He keeps us together—heart, body, soul, mind, and spirit.

Lean your entire self upon Him, and soon your stress will disappear in the power of His love and light.

I'm depending on You, Lord, for all I need. You've
brought me out of the depths of despair so many
times before. Do so again as I lean back on You.

FIRST NECESSITY

If you seek Him [inquiring for and of Him, craving Him
as your soul's first necessity], He will be found by you.
2 CHRONICLES 15:2 AMPC

The Spirit of God came on Azariah and he spoke to King Asa. He told him how in times past, "there was no peace to him who went out nor to him who came in, but great and vexing afflictions and disturbances were upon all the inhabitants" (verse 5 AMPC). (Sound familiar?) But if he, and they, went seeking God, they would find Him. "Be strong, therefore," said Azariah, "and let not your hands be weak and slack, for your work shall be rewarded" (verse 7 AMPC).

When you have nothing but trouble, when stress is weighing you down, immobilizing you from doing anything for God, seek Him. You'll find Him waiting to hear your voice and to give you peace of mind, body, spirit, and soul.

Lord, I come seeking Your face, craving Your presence
above all else. Give me the peace only You can give.
Then strengthen my hands to do Your will.

SING ALONG

The Lord your God is in the midst of you, a Mighty One, a Savior [Who saves]! He will rejoice over you with joy; He will rest [in silent satisfaction] and in His love He will be silent and make no mention [of past sins, or even recall them].
ZEPHANIAH 3:17 AMPC

When you're writing an email, it's easy enough to fix and forget your mistakes by hitting the DELETE button. If you're using a pencil to work out a math problem, an eraser rectifies any errors. But you may find it more difficult to fix and forget the mistakes you make in what you say or do in your life.

Yet God wants you to know that when you've misstepped and asked Him for forgiveness, He not only doesn't bring up your errors but forgets all about them! And He "exult[s] over you with singing" (Zephaniah 3:17 AMPC)!

So don't worry about your past mistakes. Forget about them, just like God has. Then join in the singing!

Thank You for always forgiving me when I mess up, Lord. Lead me in song with You!

FROM GROAN TO GOOD

*The Holy Spirit helps us in our weakness. For example,
we don't know what God wants us to pray for.
But the Holy Spirit prays for us with groanings
that cannot be expressed in words.*

ROMANS 8:26 NLT

Amid a stressful situation or a crisis, our emotions threaten to take over. Thoughts scatter. Hearts thump out of control. We cannot find our voices or even utter a sane word. That's when God's Spirit steps in and rescues us.

In these moments, we don't have the strength or calm to zero in on what God wants us to pray for. But it doesn't matter. All we need to do is moan and groan, and we trigger the Holy Spirit who prays *for us*! And God, who knows our hearts, will "get" it. He'll "get" us. He'll examine our situation and work out whatever's happening for good.

*Sometimes I feel so helpless, Spirit,
so wordless. But You know me. You see me.
Be my Comforter, my Messenger. Tell God all
about it. Turn my groan into something good.*

GOD'S A KEEPER

I, the Lord, am its Keeper; I water it every moment;
lest anyone harm it, I guard and keep it night and day.
ISAIAH 27:3 AMPC

You're someone the Lord has planted in this time, in this place, in this world. And your Father God has promised to tend you, to water you with love, compassion, mercy, forgiveness, and grace. He'll send His angels to guard and protect you while you're awake and when you sleep. There's nothing He won't do to keep you safe and close to Him. That's His part to play. Yours is to keep yourself close to Him.

To do that, immerse yourself in His Word, breathe in His presence, seek His face, and speak to Him through prayer. Be the flower He has created you to be, the lily that has no worries for she knows her gardener is in her midst. And when you do, you will find yourself not stressed but blooming where you are planted.

Lord, You're my Keeper, constantly tending to me,
protecting me. Help me to bloom where You've
planted me—for Your glory!

GOD QUIETS POUNDING WAVES

You faithfully answer our prayers with awesome deeds,
O God our savior. You are the hope of everyone on
earth. . . . You formed the mountains by your power
and armed yourself with mighty strength. You quieted
the raging oceans with their pounding waves.
PSALM 65:5–7 NLT

You may have some worries that are deeply rooted. They're old and full of power, keeping you from easily being freed of them. That's when you need to reach out more than once (perhaps multiple times) and call on God, the Master of awesome deeds.

God has not only formed all that you see around you—including you—but all that lies beyond you in this world and the next. He is a supernatural being with more power than you can even begin to imagine. Trust Him to quiet those waves of worries deep within you. To stop them from pounding upon your inner spirit. To extinguish them altogether.

Pray, and God will faithfully answer with awesome deeds.

Lord, free me of the power of this worry. . . .
My hope lies in You alone.

YOU CHOOSE

*"Today I am giving you a choice between life and death,
between prosperity and disaster. For I command you this
day to love the LORD your God and to keep his commands,
decrees, and regulations by walking in his ways."*

DEUTERONOMY 30:15–16 NLT

Each day God gives you a choice between life with less stress
or deathlike life with more stress. To have the former, simply
love God, do as He commands, and walk on the path He has
set before you. "If you do this, you will live and multiply, and
the LORD your God will bless you and the land you are about
to enter and occupy" (Deuteronomy 30:16 NLT). But if you
choose the latter, if you decide to serve other, lesser gods (such
as money, pride, greed, envy, etc.), you will find a much harder
road ahead and a zombielike existence.

God has given His people the freedom and the power of
choice. What will you choose? Whom will you serve?

*Lord, thank You for the power of choice.
I choose to serve You today!*

TURNING

Before him [Josiah] there was no king like him, who turned to the LORD with all his heart and with all his soul and with all his might, according to all the Law of Moses, nor did any like him arise after him.

2 KINGS 23:25 ESV

It's easy to get caught up in the world's wants, the media mayhem, the technology torrent, the society schism, but God wants you less stressed, turned to Him with all your heart, soul, and strength.

So today endeavor to turn away from the chaos and crisis surrounding you and lean into God. For as you "turn your eyes upon Jesus" and "look full in His wonderful face," you'll find "the things of earth will grow strangely dim, in the light of His glory and grace" (lyrics to "Turn Your Eyes upon Jesus" by Helen H. Lemmel [1922]).

*Lord, when I turn to You with all I am,
my stress fades away. So I look to You now,
Lord. Catch me up in You.*

BUILDING HOPE

*Oh! May the God of green hope fill you up
with joy, fill you up with peace, so that your
believing lives, filled with the life-giving energy
of the Holy Spirit, will brim over with hope!*
ROMANS 15:13 MSG

Dictionary.com defines *hope* as "the feeling that what is wanted can be had or that events will turn out for the best" or "grounds for this feeling in a particular instance." That's an awesome quality to acquire, for it seems hope would naturally ward off worry!

Make it your aim to build up your hope in God. Scour the Bible for verses about hope. Memorize them, perhaps beginning with today's verse. Or maybe Psalm 42:5 (ESV): "Why are you cast down, O my soul, and why are you in turmoil within me? Hope in God; for I shall again praise him."

Remember, you are the daughter of the King, the Master, the Creator who has "plans to give you a future filled with hope" (Jeremiah 29:11 GW).

*God of hope, fill me up with Your joy and peace
so that I'll be brimming over with hope!*

TAKE YOUR STAND

During the night an angel of God opened the jailhouse door and led them out. He said, "Go to the Temple and take your stand. Tell the people. . .about this Life." Promptly obedient, they entered the Temple at daybreak and went on with their teaching.

ACTS 5:19–20 MSG

In the same way God's angel rescued the apostles—even while men stood guard—God can rescue you from whatever has you imprisoned. Yet He doesn't help you escape so you can spend more time watching TV. He wants you to be obedient to what He would have you do.

God has given you life for a reason. He has a calling for you. Once you have made Jesus Lord of your life, it's time to be free, to be brave, to have peace in Him, and to be obedient to His voice. He wants you to take your stand and share His life with others.

Lord, break my soul out of its imprisonment. Help me to rise above my stress so I can make the wonders of Your way and life known to others, freeing them for You.

Day 263

ON PURPOSE

O God. . . . I will hide beneath the shadow of your wings until the danger passes by. I cry out to God Most High. . .who will fulfill his purpose for me. He will send help from heaven to rescue me.
PSALM 57:1–3 NLT

When we're on the run, feeling as if troubles are chasing us down, there's only one place to go. To God, the One we trust with all our being. When the storms, the hawk, or the wolf is on our tail, we can be as chicks who scramble to hunker down under the wings of their mother hen, confident she will keep them whole, warm, and dry. We're confident God won't let us down, that He will send help from heaven to pluck us out of trouble, because He has a plan, a purpose for our life.

When stress prowls around your door, run to God. Hide in Him until the storm passes. Then live your purpose—on purpose.

Here I come, Lord, taking refuge beneath
Your wings until I have the courage to
walk Your way once again.

OUT OF THE PIT

"I called out your name, O God, called from the bottom of the pit. You listened when I called out, 'Don't shut your ears! Get me out of here! Save me!' You came close when I called out. You said, 'It's going to be all right.' "
Lamentations 3:56–57 MSG

When your worries have you feeling as if you're at the bottom of a dark pit, your avenue back into the light is to call out from the depths. Call God by one of the many names that describe His character and fit your need—God Almighty, Defender, Strong Tower, the God Who Watches Over Me, Refuge, Shield, the Lord My Rock, Lord of Light.

Know that God *will* hear you and listen to what you say. He *will* get you out of the depths of darkness and into His light. As He sidles up next to you, you'll hear His reassuring words, "It's going to be all right."

Lord of Light and Life, free me from this pit of worry! Come close when I call!

AS HIGH AS THE HEAVENS

*My heart is confident in you, O God. . . . No wonder
I can sing your praises! Wake up, my heart! Wake up,
O lyre and harp! I will wake the dawn with my
song. . . . I will sing your praises. . . . For your
unfailing love is as high as the heavens.*
PSALM 57:7–10 NLT

A great way to beat stress is to fall asleep with an uplifting, confidence-supplying Bible verse in your mind. A verse that gives your heart strength and peace, allowing not only for a restful night but a joyful morning. Wouldn't it be wonderful to be singing praises to God upon waking rather than rehearsing problems in your mind?

Try claiming a life-giving promise or truth about God or His love and faithfulness before you close your eyes. And discover how much your stress lessens and your praises increase, reaching "as high as the heavens."

*Lord, give me a verse to fall asleep to, one that, with
the morning light, will help my heart take flight.*

NOT STRESSED BUT BLESSED

*And blessed (happy, to be envied) is she who believed
that there would be a fulfillment of the things that
were spoken to her from the Lord.*
LUKE 1:45 AMPC

How blessed was Mary because she believed God could do the impossible—for her and her cousin Elizabeth. Mary believed the angel Gabriel when he told her she had nothing to fear (see verse 30). That she would become pregnant without having slept with a man and that her son Jesus would be God's Son (see verses 34–35). That her aged cousin Elizabeth would become pregnant in her old age (see verse 36). That nothing was impossible with God (see verse 37).

Happy will you be if you believe God's promises to you and submit to Him, loving Him and serving Him, as Mary did.

*I am Your servant, Lord, and I believe You will
make Your promises come true in my life. Because
of these two things, I am not stressed but blessed!
May everything You have said come true.
For everything is possible with You!*

GOD PLANS GOOD

"Even though you planned evil against me,
God planned good to come out of it.
This was to keep many people alive,
as he is doing now."
GENESIS 50:20 GW

Joseph was the favored son of his father, Jacob. One day, out of jealousy, Joseph's brothers threw him into a pit then sold him to traders. He was bought by an officer of Pharaoh of Egypt, unjustly accused of rape, and thrown into a dungeon. Yet through all these things, Joseph never worried but trusted in God. No matter what happened or where he landed, "The LORD was with Joseph, so he became a successful man" (Genesis 39:2 GW) and eventually was made the number two man in Egypt. As such, he was able to save his family.

Even though you may be going through some tough times, don't worry. Trust that God has a purpose for you. No matter what happens, have faith that God is planning good to come out of it. And you too will be successful.

Thank You, Lord, for loving me. I'm trusting
in Your purposes, knowing You're
planning something good.

BLESSINGS ABOUND

"I belong to the Lord, body and soul," replied Mary,
"let it happen as you say." And at this the angel left her.
LUKE 1:38 PHILLIPS

How readily do you submit to the Lord, give Him ownership over you? How much you submit to God directly correlates to how much you truly trust Him—to do what He says He will do in His Word, to stick to His promises, to work out all things for your good, to overcome the darkness that seems determined to surround you, and to lead you into the light.

Build up your trust in God by keeping track of answered prayers, by recounting your blessings before bed, and by memorizing and expecting His promises as recorded in the Bible. For when you give all of yourself to God, when you let go and let God, blessings begin to abound.

Help me, Lord, to give up all of myself and my life
to You so that I can fully become Your obedient
daughter, confident in and blessed by You.

FOUR WAYS

*Delight yourselves in God, yes, find your joy in
him at all times. Have a reputation for gentleness,
and never forget the nearness of your Lord.*

PHILIPPIANS 4:4–5 PHILLIPS

This scripture covers at least four ways to keep stress at bay. The first is to delight yourself in God. Revel in His Word. Take pleasure just being in His company. The second is to find your joy in the Lord at all times! Look for Him hiding around the corner. Laugh when He works things out beyond anything you could have imagined. See Him in the smile of a stranger. The third is to be known for your gentleness. People admire the soft-spoken, those who exhibit contentment no matter what is happening in their lives. And the last is to "never forget the nearness of your Lord." Knowing He is right beside you, loving you, protecting you, delighting in you, is a wonderful thing to keep in the forefront of your mind, just as He keeps you in the forefront of His.

*Lord, thank You for bringing such joy
and delight into my life!*

A HOME BUILDER

A wise woman builds her home, but a foolish
woman tears it down with her own hands.
PROVERBS 14:1 NLT

Worry has a domino effect. If you start fretting over something that has caught your attention and then voice it or act panic-stricken, chances are others around you will fall in with your anxiety. Everyone in your household, church, or workplace will come unglued.

Better to be a wise woman who builds up her home and her fellow travelers with a steady life of prayer and encouragement as well as an evident faith in God. When worries enter your thoughts, seek Jesus' face immediately. Ask Him to take on your troubles as you pick up His peace. Trust that He will see you through no matter what lies ahead or behind. Then you will be in a position to help others work through their own worries, mostly by being a calm, good listener, encouraging them when they need it, and giving wise advice when asked.

Lord, help me be a wise woman, building up my home
by giving You my worries and taking on Your peace.

LEARN TO BE CONTENT

I have learned to be content, whatever the circumstances
may be. I know now how to live when things are
difficult and I know how to live when things are
prosperous. In general and in particular I have learned
the secret of facing either poverty or plenty.
PHILIPPIANS 4:11–12 PHILLIPS

How simple it was for us to be content when we were younger.
Our tears, if any, lasted only until we got our crayon back, were
eating our favorite cookie, saw our mother's smile, or heard our
father's laugh. It was those simple things that made us happy.

Why not have that attitude now? Practice finding joy and
contentment in the simple things life gives you—a sunset, a
fallen leaf, a flower petal, a smile from a loved one, a good book,
a soft song, a call from a friend. . . The list could go on and on.

Learn to be content and your stress will have no place to
hang its hat.

Help me, Lord, to find contentment in the
little things—all of which are Your miracles.

THE RIGHT SPIRIT

*We can be full of joy here and now even in our trials
and troubles. Taken in the right spirit these very things
will give us patient endurance; this in turn will develop
a mature character, and a character of this sort produces
a steady hope, a hope that will never disappoint us.*
ROMANS 5:3–4 PHILLIPS

Being joyful is a matter of choice. It depends on how we choose
to respond to the things that come our way. With the right
spirit, we'll find a way to patiently endure. Having the right
spirit will help us to grow up into God and develop a character
marked by a steady hope.

What's happening in your life right now? What's your attitude toward it? Are you looking for the blessing—no matter
how small—amid the trouble?

If you feel stuck in your current attitude or perspective, take
a moment each night to write down five good things happening
in your life, and watch how that practice will revive your spirit.

*Lord, help me to have the right spirit—
no matter what's happening in my life!*

CELEBRATE TOGETHER

"The master was full of praise. 'Well done, my good and faithful servant. You have been faithful in handling this small amount, so now I will give you many more responsibilities. Let's celebrate together!'"

MATTHEW 25:21 NLT

When you've accomplished something good, no matter how big or little, take time to celebrate. Look up to God, thanking Him for His help. Know that He will be full of praise for you. He will be giving you an "atta girl" for a job well done. For in all you do, you aren't really serving other people but Him, your Master!

As you continue to handle the little things well, God will give you more things to do. But the main point here is to take time to celebrate with God. Pause in His presence and pleasure. Know He is watching you, that He approves you and sees you as faithful and praiseworthy. Then praise Him back!

I'm so excited to celebrate with You today, Lord! What shall we tackle together next?

RIGHT INTENTIONS

*Aim at and pursue righteousness (all
that is virtuous and good, right living,
conformity to the will of God in thought,
word, and deed); [and aim at and
pursue] faith, love, [and] peace.*

2 TIMOTHY 2:22 AMPC

Setting your aims or intentions for the day (or your life) before your feet hit the floor may keep you from easily slipping into worry. So, you *can* intend to not worry. But rather than going with a negative, why not set a positive intention that will leave no room for fretting. Consider what the apostle Paul tells Timothy to intend: "aim at and pursue" living God's way and go after "faith, love, [and] peace." No worries there!

Today, before you rise from your bed, make it your intention to live right, the way God would have you live. Make up your mind to pursue faith, love, and peace, and worry will lose its foothold. The intentions you set are usually met.

*Today, Lord, my intention is to pursue faith, love,
and peace with You by my side!*

LIGHTEN UP

*But he's already made it plain how to live, what to do,
what GOD is looking for in. . .women. It's quite simple:
Do what is fair and just to your neighbor,
be compassionate and loyal in your love, and don't
take yourself too seriously—take God seriously.*
MICAH 6:8 MSG

One of the best ways to de-stress is to get out of your own head by doing something for someone else. You may think that you don't have the time or energy to help a neighbor, babysit the child of a harassed mom, or visit an elderly woman in her retirement home. Or maybe you think you're already doing so much for everyone else in your life, you can't possibly carve out five more minutes to serve anyone else.

But when you do something for someone else outside of your usual routine, the benefits far outweigh any time or effort you expend. God is looking for you to lighten up about your own life and invest yourself in Him.

*Help me get out of my own head today, Lord.
Show me who to love.*

YOUR GUIDE AND GUARDIAN

"He found them in a. . .howling wasteland. He surrounded them and watched over them; he guarded them as he would guard his own eyes. Like an eagle that. . .hovers over her young, so he spread his wings to take them up and carried them safely on his pinions."
DEUTERONOMY 32:10–11 NLT

Sometimes you may feel as if you're all alone in a desert, lost and unprotected, the wind howling all around you. You worry that you're too vulnerable, that there's no one able to help you.

Rest easy. God is with you. He's surrounding you, watching over you. He's guarding you as if you were the apple or pupil of His eyes. He knows how fragile you can be and promises to protect you. Like a mother eagle, He's spreading His wings over you. He'll take you up and carry you, leading you to a better place where His promises will override your worries.

Thank You, Lord, for coming to meet me where I am. Guard me as You do Your own eyes. Carry me away to Your land of promise.

ROCK OUT

Speak out to one another in psalms and hymns and
spiritual songs, offering praise with voices [and
instruments] and making melody with all your heart to
the Lord, at all times and for everything giving thanks
in the name of our Lord Jesus Christ to God the Father.
EPHESIANS 5:19–20 AMPC

Another way to de-stress by getting out of your own head is to exchange your mental machinations for God's. You can do that by singing praises to Him. Make melody with all you are, your mind, body, heart, and soul—no matter how off-key you might be! Singing God's praises and giving Him thanks for all the blessings He has bestowed upon you will lift your entire being, drawing you closer to the place He would have you be. You'll not only be uplifted but gain all the strength and energy you need to continue on.

So what are you waiting for? Find a praise tune and rock out—for the Rock!

Lord, thank You so much for all You've done for me.
I lift my eyes and praise to You.

MIGHTY POWER

Now all glory to God, who is able, through his mighty power at work within us, to accomplish infinitely more than we might ask or think.
EPHESIANS 3:20 NLT

Imagine it. God working so deeply within you. His creative power giving you the strength, the determination, the skill, the resources, the energy to do everything He has purposed you to do! And the means and ways to do it far beyond what you ever thought you could accomplish *in your wildest dreams and imagination*. He has given you power to do things you haven't even dared ask!

God has planted you in this world to do something marvelous and works through you to finish that job. You have all you require. So don't stress. Realize how blessed and power-filled you are as you live your life for His will and glory!

I am amazed, Lord, at how much You have equipped me to do what You would have me do. Thank You for Your mighty power working through me to bring You glory!

YOUR BEST DEFENSE

*The Lord is my Rock, my Fortress, and my
Deliverer; my God, my keen and firm Strength in
Whom I will trust and take refuge, my Shield, and
the Horn of my salvation, my High Tower.*
PSALM 18:2 AMPC

If you're looking for a defense against worry, look no further than your Lord. That's what David did, and he became the apple of God's eye (see Psalm 17:8 ESV) even when and after he made some pretty major mistakes!

In Psalm 18, David begins by telling God how much he loves Him (see Psalm 18:1). Then he describes what God is to him—his Rock, Fortress, Deliverer, Strength, Shield, Horn (power), and High Tower. Then, he sings, "I will call upon the Lord, Who is to be praised; so shall I be saved from my enemies" (Psalm 18:3 AMPC).

When worry gets out of hand, keeping you from doing what God would have you do, sing a song of praise to Him. Remind yourself of who He is, and He will save you!

*My Rock and Deliverer, save me from my
worries as I sing a song of praise to You!*

ACCORDING TO YOUR NEED

*This is what the Lord has commanded: Let every
man gather of it as much as he will need. . . . When
they measured it. . .he who gathered much had
nothing over, and he who gathered little had no
lack; each gathered according to his need.*
EXODUS 16:16, 18 AMPC

God knows exactly what you need. He has promised to provide
it. Your job is to trust He will do so. For when you begin to
doubt that the One who created you and everything around
you is going to be there for you, stress and anxiety quickly
set in. You begin trying to provide everything you need all by
yourself, leaving God out of the equation entirely. So stop. Take
stock of what you've taken on, how much you're straining to
gather "just in case." Bring the Great Provider back into the
equation. Know that with the Good Shepherd first in your life,
you can relax and say:

*The Lord is my Shepherd [to feed, guide,
and shield me], I shall not lack (Psalm 23:1 AMPC).*

— Day 281 —

ULTIMATE STAIN REMOVER

*For his unfailing love toward those who fear
him is as great as the height of the heavens
above the earth. He has removed our sins as
far from us as the east is from the west.*
PSALM 103:11–12 NLT

God's unfathomable amount of love for you is the one constant in your life. Although at times you may not understand why certain things happen, you can always rest assured God will never leave or forsake you. Because you recognize Him as the Master and Creator and worship Him first in your life, you can be assured of the greatness of His love for you. In fact, His love is so huge that He has forgiven *and forgotten* every mistake you've made, every offense you've committed. He has removed them from you as far as "the east is from the west." That's a forever thing, an eternal promise.

So stress no longer over past misdeeds. God has already forgotten them. Instead, rest in Him, knowing you're forever loved and forgiven.

*You, Lord, are the ultimate Stain Remover.
Thank You for loving me so much.*

BLESSED IN ASTONISHING WAYS

God can pour on the blessings in
astonishing ways so that you're ready for
anything and everything, more than just
ready to do what needs to be done.
2 Corinthians 9:8 msg

George Müller ran an orphanage in England in the 1800s. One morning, there was no money, and the children's breakfast bowls and cups were empty. As the kids stood, waiting for their meal, Müller prayed, "Dear Father, we thank Thee for what Thou art going to give us to eat."

Then a baker, prompted by God, knocked on the door. His arms were filled with bread for the children. He was followed by a milkman whose cart had broken down in front of the orphanage. He wanted to give the kids cans of milk so he could empty and repair his wagon.

God knows and has what you need. Transform your worries about want into prayers for provisions, and you'll be blessed "in astonishing ways."

Lord, bless me in astonishing ways so that
I may bless others in return.

BEARING UP

I have loved you with an everlasting love; therefore with loving-kindness have I drawn you and continued My faithfulness to you. Again I will build you and you will be built. . . ! You will again. . .go forth in the dancing [chorus] of those who make merry.

JEREMIAH 31:3–4 AMPC

Nothing can shake you up more than a situation—a word, a look, a loss—you didn't see coming, prompting you to react automatically by fight, flight, or freeze. Those are the times when any other little annoyance or problem added to that unexpected event makes the stress almost unbearable.

The key is to remember God loves you. He has called you, drawn you to Him so He can help you. He has given you promises to rise up on, words to stand on, hope to heal. This too shall pass. And, though it may not seem possible now, day by day the pain will abate until you find joy in life and in the Lord once again.

Lord, help me to bear up. Be faithful in carrying me as I faithfully put my hope in You.

RECALL, RECOUNT, PRONOUNCE

The Lord, the God of heaven, Who took me. . .from the land of my family and my birth, Who spoke to me and swore to me, saying, To your offspring I will give this land—He will send His Angel before you, and you will take a wife from there for my son.

GENESIS 24:7 AMPC

The clock was ticking. Time was of the essence when an old Abraham, showing great trust in God, sent his servant to find a wife for his son Isaac. Abraham recalled how God had led him away from home to a foreign land of His choosing. He recounted the promise God had made, saying this land would be his children's. And now Abraham pronounces his belief that God will send His angel before his servant as he embarks upon this wife-seeking journey.

To become as trusting as Abraham, recall how God has led you. Recount the promises He has made to you. Pronounce your belief that God is sending His angels ahead of you.

Lead me on, Lord. Though I know not where, I trust in You.

KINGDOM-OF-HEAVEN BLESSING

Even if you suffer for doing what is right, God will reward
you for it. So don't worry or be afraid of their threats.
Instead, you must worship Christ as Lord of your life.
1 Peter 3:14–15 nlt

Today's verse, which says you're not to worry or be afraid when you're threatened, was written by the disciple Peter, who'd been both worried and afraid when Jesus was arrested. In fact, he went so far as to deny even knowing Jesus! But in the end, Peter was more devoted to Jesus than ever.

Jesus doesn't promise you a life without trouble, but He does promise you His peace and reward if you stick close to Him, doing what's right.

When you feel threatened by what others say and do as you live for Jesus, just keep Him and His words set in your mind and heart. Worship instead of worry, assured of your reward and God's kingdom-of-heaven blessing (see Matthew 5:10).

With You as my Lord and fortress, I need not
worry or fear the words of others. Thank You,
Lord, for blessing me as I follow You.

Day 286
REQUEST SUCCESS

*So humble yourselves under the mighty power of God,
and at the right time he will lift you up in honor. Give all
your worries and cares to God, for he cares about you.*
1 PETER 5:6–7 NLT

Abraham's servant sets off on his master's mission. After arriving at his destination, he stops and prays for guidance, saying, "O LORD, God of my master, Abraham. . . . Please give me success today, and show unfailing love to my master, Abraham. See, I am standing here beside this spring, and the young women of the town are coming out to draw water. This is my request. . . ." (Genesis 24:12–14 NLT).

Instead of stressing out, allowing what-ifs to clamor around in his head, this dedicated and trustworthy servant stopped and prayed for guidance, outlining his and his master's situations and asking for success—and got it!

Stop. Pray for guidance. Present your situation to the Lord. Ask Him for success. And rise with peace, knowing your life is in good hands.

*Lord of lords, here's my request. . . .
Please grant me success!*

Day 287

READY, WILLING, AND ABLE

"So today when I came to the spring, I prayed. . . .
Before I had finished praying in my heart,
I saw Rebekah. . . ."
GENESIS 24:42, 45 NLT

Before Abraham's servant had even finished praying his prayer, God answered it in the form of Rebekah, who then became Isaac's wife! As soon as the servant realized Rebekah fit all of Abraham's requirements for his son Isaac, "the man bowed low and worshiped the LORD" (Genesis 24:26 NLT).

God is ready, willing, and able to answer your prayers the same way. He has given you the promise, "I will answer them before they even call to me. While they are still talking about their needs, I will go ahead and answer their prayers!" (Isaiah 65:24 NLT). And once your prayers are answered, respond like Abraham's humble servant. Bow and worship your good Lord.

Lord, You amaze me. You answer my prayers before
I even approach You. Yet You still want me
to say the words, to pray from my heart.
So here I am, Lord. I pray. . .

CHIN UP, WOMAN!

Energize the limp hands, strengthen the rubbery knees.
Tell fearful souls, "Courage! Take heart! GOD is here,
right here, on his way to put things right and redress
all wrongs. He's on his way! He'll save you!"
ISAIAH 35:3–4 MSG

It's good to have some Bible verses memorized, ones you can just call up during times of worry, stress, fear, or crises. Isaiah 35:3–4 are two of these verses. Find a Bible version of them that really speaks to your heart. Then use it when you start feeling anxious, when your hands are weak and your knees are about to give way.

Speak Isaiah's words into your soul to strengthen your body, mind, and spirit, rephrasing them if you need to. Say to yourself, "Chin up, woman. Be brave. Take heart. God is right here with you. He's going to put things right. He's on His way to save you!"

Remember, Jesus is your Immanuel, which means "God is with us" (Matthew 1:23 MSG)! So don't panic—pray!!!

Thank God You're with me, Jesus! With You heading
my way, I know You'll put things right!

PERSISTENCE

But David persisted.
1 SAMUEL 17:34 NLT

Sometimes we find ourselves stressing out because we believe we're not doing what God has called us to do. In effect, we're just spinning our wheels, leading the lives others expect us to lead.

Before becoming king, David went to visit his brothers, found out about the taunts of Goliath, and figured he'd fight the giant no one else was willing to face. His brother got angry and told him to go back to tending sheep. But David stayed. Later King Saul told him, "You can't fight this giant. You're just a kid with no battle experience."

"But David persisted," claiming he'd already killed bears and lions to protect his father's sheep and goats, saying, "The LORD who rescued me from the claws of the lion and the bear will rescue me from this Philistine!" (1 Samuel 17:37 NLT).

Consider the naysayers and discouragers in your own life. Consider what God has been training you for. Then ask. . .

Lord, what's Your dream for my life? What calling would You have me persist in?

Day 290
EQUIPMENT

He picked up five smooth stones from a stream and put them into his shepherd's bag. Then, armed only with his shepherd's staff and sling, he started across the valley to fight the Philistine.
1 SAMUEL 17:40 NLT

Once Saul was convinced David might have a chance against the giant, he determined to outfit David, putting his own armor on the boy. But once the gear was on, David could barely walk. So he told Saul, "I can't go in these. . . . I'm not used to them" (verse 39 NLT), and took the equipment off. David then went off to face Goliath, equipped with a few stones, his staff, and a sling, fully assured he would succeed in the power of God.

God has made you special, equipping you with simple tools that fit you personally and giving you the confidence that you'll succeed in *His* power.

Help me de-stress, Lord, by exchanging this equipment that doesn't fit me for the special gear You've fashioned just for me to meet my challenges, enabling me to succeed in Your power, not my own.

NEVER SHAKEN

I will bless the L<small>ORD</small> who guides me; even at night my heart instructs me. I know the L<small>ORD</small> is always with me. I will not be shaken, for he is right beside me.

P<small>SALM</small> 16:7–8 <small>NLT</small>

These days, lots of businesses are open 24–7. But God has been open and available to His people day and night since they were created.

So if you have the all-powerful Creator constantly by your side, guiding you in the day and advising you in the night, whatever could you be worried about?

See things through God's eternal perspective. Your days are like a moment to Him. So live life to the fullest with no worries, fears, or anxieties to distract you or to keep you from the joy and peace that is yours in Christ.

God is with you. You will never be shaken. Let that stir your spirit into moving in rhythm with Him, filled with courage, peace, and joy, all the days of your life.

I bless You, Lord, for guiding me, teaching me, and always being with me. I need not be shaken because You're beside me!

TIMING

He waited seven days, the time appointed by Samuel.
But Samuel did not come to Gilgal, and the people
were scattering from him. So Saul. . .offered the burnt
offering. As soon as he had finished offering the
burnt offering, behold, Samuel came.
1 Samuel 13:8–10 esv

The prophet Samuel had told Saul to wait for him in Gilgal.
When Samuel got there, he would make a sacrifice and tell
Saul God's will for him. But Saul, reacting to the fear of the
troops who were with him, decided to take matters into his
own hands. The result of his bowing to circumstances instead
of being obedient to and trusting God was that Saul's kingdom
would cease and the Lord would assign a "man after his own
heart" (verse 14 esv) to rule His people.

God has His own particular timing for every event in your
life. So don't stress. Be a woman after God's own heart. And
may your prayer be this:

I wait for the Lord, my soul waits,
and in his word I hope (Psalm 130:5 esv).

TIME AND PLACE

The Lord gave this message to Jonah son of Amittai:
"Get up and go to the great city of Nineveh. . . ."
But Jonah got up and went in the opposite direction
to get away from the Lord. . . . Then Jonah prayed
to the Lord his God from inside the fish.
Jonah 1:1–3; 2:1 nlt

Being in the wrong place at the wrong time can cause major stress. Jonah found that out when God told him to go one way and he headed in the opposite direction. Not only did the prophet end up on a ship during a terrible storm, but he ultimately landed in the belly of a whale. It was only after that whale vomited him back onto the shore that Jonah headed in God's direction.

Which way do you head when God asks you to "get up and go"?

Lord, You know where I am in my life. Show me the
next steps. Lead me where You want me to go
so that I'm walking in Your will and Your way.

PARTNERING WITH GOD

We are assured and know that [God being a partner
in their labor] all things work together and are [fitting
into a plan] for good to and for those who love God and
are called according to [His] design and purpose.
ROMANS 8:28 AMPC

Romans 8:28 says that everything that happens in your life—whether good or bad, within or out of your control—happens for a reason and according to God's plan and that He will make everything work out for your good.

That can be hard to accept sometimes, yet that doesn't mean it isn't true. After all, it was true for Joseph, who'd been put in a pit by loved ones, sold as a slave, sent to the dungeon, and yet ended up the number two man in Egypt!

Instead of worrying about what may or may not happen, rest in the assurance that no matter what happens, God will work it out for good. Remember, God can do anything. Your job? Trust Him.

Lord, with You as my partner, I know all things will
work out for good. On that I stake my faith!

Day 295

THE RIGHT EQUIPMENT, TIME, AND PLACE

*"If you keep silent at this time, relief and deliverance
will rise for the Jews from another place. . . .
And who knows whether you have not come
to the kingdom for such a time as this?"*
ESTHER 4:14 ESV

Esther had the right equipment to land her in the king's harem.
And she was in exactly the right place when a major threat arose
against God's people. Although she found herself caught amid
the machinations of men, her cousin gave her some sage advice,
telling her that perhaps she was in this time and place for a reason. That God would work through her to deliver His people.

Queen Esther rose above the stressful situation by remaining faithful. She ordered a fast to help ensure success then put
herself and the situation in God's hands, knowing the results
would be according to His will.

*You've equipped me, Lord, for a purpose.
Show me what You would have me do in this
time and place. I leave it all in Your hands.*

POWERFUL WORD

*God means what he says. What he
says goes. His powerful Word is sharp
as a surgeon's scalpel, cutting through
everything, whether doubt or defense,
laying us open to listen and obey.*
HEBREWS 4:12 MSG

Stressed or distressed? Say a heartfelt prayer then dive deep into God's Word. It's alive and powerful, "making it active, operative, energizing, and effective" (Hebrews 4:12 AMPC). It'll go deep within, revealing what needs to be revealed. It'll give you guidance, wisdom, strength, knowledge. It'll pull you out of your present state, nurture and heal you where you need it the most. It'll give you a rock to stand on and the faith and courage to lean on God, trusting Him to carry you when you can no longer walk.

Find a verse that speaks to your heart. Then pray those words back to the Author, the Mighty One who dwells within you and invites you to shelter in His embrace.

*Nothing is more powerful than Your Word, Lord.
Tell me what I need to hear, then listen as I
whisper those words back to You.*

IN GOD'S HANDS

*God is our refuge and strength, always ready to
help in times of trouble. So we will not fear when
earthquakes come and the mountains crumble
into the sea. Let the oceans roar and foam. Let the
mountains tremble as the waters surge!*

PSALM 46:1–3 NLT

Sometimes it may feel as if your world is falling apart—literally! The weather has turned wacky; mountainous glaciers are melting, volcanoes erupting, cities flooding, forests burning. . . . It's enough to make any normal woman worry.

Yet, because you're a daughter of the Most High God, you don't have to be anxious or fear anything because you can go to God for refuge. In Him you will find all the strength and help you need to get through anything and everything.

So rest easy. Pray to God. Tell Him you know He's in control and somehow everything will be all right. You don't need to know the details. Leave them—and everything else that's on your mind—in His hands.

*Thank You, Lord, for always being there, ready to
shield, strengthen, and help me. Because of
You I have peace and courage!*

DRAW NEAR TO GOD

*Without faith it is impossible to please and be
satisfactory to Him. For whoever would come near to
God must [necessarily] believe that God exists and that
He is the rewarder of those who earnestly and
diligently seek Him [out].*
HEBREWS 11:6 AMPC

The nearer you draw to God, the further you move away from
stress. It's a fact. But when you draw near, you have to believe
that God exists and that He will reward your faith by staying
true to His promises.

Go deeper. Read about the heroes of faith in Hebrews 11.
There you will discover how faith "prompted" Noah, Abraham,
Jacob, Moses, and Rahab (verses 7, 9, 21, 23, 31). It "urged on"
Abraham (verse 8), gave Isaac visionary "eyes" (verse 20), and
gave Sarah "physical power" (verse 11). It "actuated" Joseph
(verse 22) and "aroused" and "motivated" Moses (verses 24,
27). (See AMPC.)

Faith is living and active. Draw near to God, the ultimate
Promise Keeper and Faith Maker.

*Lord, I'm coming close, relying on Your
promises. Move me with faith—prompt me,
urge me on, inspire me to live for You.*

RISING UP

Those who wait for the Lord [who expect, look for, and hope in Him] shall change and renew their strength and power; they shall lift their wings and mount up [close to God] as eagles [mount up to the sun]; they shall run and not be weary, they shall walk and not faint or become tired.

ISAIAH 40:31 AMPC

When stress seems to have gotten the best of you, the words of Isaiah 40:31 will help you pull your eyes off yourself and lift them to the Lord. So look up. Know God is on your side. Be patiently expectant, knowing He will come through for you. He already has a plan. In fact, He's working things out behind the scenes. He will fill you with strength and power to meet the challenges and opportunities in front of you.

So open up your wings. Take a deep breath and see yourself rising up to Him, as close as you can get. Feel the stress fall away as you head for the Son.

I'm rising up to You, Lord.

PULLED BY PROMISES

*With promises like this to pull us on, dear friends,
let's make a clean break with everything that defiles or
distracts us, both within and without. Let's make our
entire lives fit and holy temples for the worship of God.*

2 CORINTHIANS 7:1 MSG

God has a plan for your life. He wants you to live for Him, to trust Him, to base your words and actions on His promises, to expect good to come out of all things.

God wants you, His darling daughter, to be strong and fit. For that, you need "a calm and undisturbed mind and heart," which are "the life and health of the body" (Proverbs 14:30 AMPC).

For God's pleasure and your own health and welfare, make a clean break from the worries that distract you. Go to God, trusting Him with your concerns. Dig into His promises, believing them and making them your own. Live in God's reality, and you'll be living the life He dreamed for you.

*Help me be a fit temple for You, Lord.
Give me the calm mind I yearn for in You.*

Day 301

PRAY, THEN PRY

Behold, I stand at the door and knock;
if anyone hears and listens to and heeds My
voice and opens the door, I will come in to him.
REVELATION 3:20 AMPC

When you're in the midst of a stressful situation, getting yourself
to sit down and pray may take some effort. But that's exactly
what Jesus is waiting for you to do. He's standing there knocking, waiting for you to open the door to His presence. Once
you do, He can then open up your heart to receive what He's
telling you.

The Lord did that for Lydia. "One of those who listened to
us was a woman named Lydia. . . . And the Lord opened her
heart to pay attention to what was said" (Acts 16:14 AMPC).
He's waiting right now to do the same for you.

Pray, then pry that door open. Let the Son's light in.

I know You're waiting, Lord. So here I am, opening
my door to You, so that You can open the door
to my heart. Speak to me, Lord.

LOVE MEETS YOU

O my Strength, I will watch for you, for you, O God, are my fortress. My God in his steadfast love will meet me.
Psalm 59:9–10 esv

Stress comes, in part, from trying to do things in your own strength. But once you acknowledge that whatever strength you have comes from God, a weight lifts. For when you feel weak, you can turn your gaze away from your worries and up to God. Set yourself to watch for your true Strength. Hang out in His fortress, His high tower. Know that no matter what the problem, situation, or circumstance, the Lord, the Prince of Peace, the mighty Spirit, is there, loving you, holding you up, empowering you. In fact, He's been watching you. He's already gone ahead to pave the way before you. Wait. Watch. His love will meet you.

Here I am, Lord, waiting, watching, knowing
You are the Prince to whom I can run,
whose love meets me where I am.

Day 303
NO LIMIT

Thanks be to God, Who gives us the victory [making us conquerors] through our Lord Jesus Christ.
1 CORINTHIANS 15:57 AMPC

The moment you feel beaten down by stress is the exact right time to remember God has already given you victory as a believer in Christ. So what is there to fear, to worry about? The One who spoke the world into being is on your side. The One who parted the Red Sea, provided manna in the wilderness, saved Daniel in the lions' den, and appeared in the midst of a fiery furnace from which three of God's people emerged unscathed. There is no limit to His strength and wisdom.

Give thanks to God right now, realizing that in Him you are more than a conqueror in this world—and the next.

Lord, write upon the walls of my mind the fact that in You, I have all the strength I need to overcome because I share the power of the One You raised up and into the light.

Day 304

CALLING AND CALMING

*"Do not be afraid or discouraged. For the L*ORD *your God is with you wherever you go."*
JOSHUA 1:9 NLT

Stress thrives when we're distracted by the world instead of focused on God's calling. Fortunately, God's Word helps us find our way out, just as He helped Joshua, the man called to lead God's people into the Promised Land. Three times, God tells Joshua to be strong and courageous. Then He tells him to obey God's Book of Instruction, meditating on it continually. For only when we make God's Word part of ourselves will we succeed in what God is calling us to do. As we hide His Word in our hearts, He promises to be with us wherever we go, making the task before us less intimidating.

Get refocused on your calling and in turn receive God's calming by spending time reading, studying, and applying the words of Joshua 1:6–9. Be strong and courageous. Live God's Word. Apply it to your life. And know God is with you.

I'm realigning my life with You, Lord. Help me find my way back to Your purpose for me.

Day 305

STAYING POWER

*Take the old prophets as your mentors. . . . What a gift
life is to those who stay the course! You've heard, of course,
of Job's staying power, and you know how God brought it
all together for him at the end. That's because God
cares, cares right down to the last detail.*
JAMES 5:11 MSG

In the short run, it may seem easy to wallow in stress, even to brag about it sometimes, saying things like, "I'm so busy I don't even have time to breathe." We seem to wear our busyness as a strange badge of honor.

But God would have us do as the old prophets did, those who "put up with anything, went through everything, and never once quit, all the time honoring God" (James 5:11 MSG). Don't let the world's woes get you down. Don't stress about what might've been. Instead, "be patient. . . . Stay steady and strong" (James 5:7 MSG). God's got you. He'll take care of everything.

*Lord, help me to stay the course, loving and serving You,
knowing You're taking care of everything.*

HEART CHECK

*"Our fathers refused to obey him, but thrust him
aside, and in their hearts they turned to Egypt,
saying to Aaron, 'Make for us gods who will go before
us. As for this Moses who led us out from the land of
Egypt, we do not know what has become of him.'"*
ACTS 7:39–40 ESV

Are you a bit stressed out? If so, look deep within. Check your
heart. Is it yearning for the comfort of the enslavement you
know? Has your heart turned to trusting in other gods—people,
money, power, possessions? Have you rejected, thrust aside, the
Lord of all, Jesus, who can help you rise above all things, who
can free you from the bondage of stress?

Determine to embrace your new life as a free woman with
the Maker of manna rather than go back to your old life as a
slave, eating the garlic and onions of Egypt.

*I'm turning my heart—as well as my mind, body,
spirit, and soul—back to You, Lord. You have
freed me to live again—forever!*

LADY-IN-WAITING

I look to you, heaven-dwelling God, look up to you for help. Like servants, alert to their master's commands, like a maiden attending her lady, we're watching and waiting, holding our breath, awaiting your word of mercy.
PSALM 123:1–2 MSG

Sometimes it takes awhile to de-stress, like air slowly leaking out of a tire. And it may take even longer for our circumstances—or we ourselves—to change. But it will happen. The key is to change your attitude. Instead of being weighed down by what isn't right, buoy yourself by being grateful for what is right. Count those blessings. Then have patience, looking up to God, watching and waiting for Him to respond to your prayers for help. Most of all, be hope-filled and alert, knowing that His word *will come* and lift your heart.

So be grateful, patient, and hopeful. Before you know it, you'll hear God whisper in your ear, telling you the word you need to hear.

Lord, I'm Your lady-in-waiting, knowing You will tell me just what I need to hear.

Day 308

MIGHTY THINGS

*Give us help for the hard task; human help
is worthless. In God we'll do our very best;
he'll flatten the opposition for good.*
PSALM 60:11–12 MSG

So many wonderful verses in the Bible give us hope and strength and help combat stress. God tells Isaiah, "Say to those who have an anxious heart, 'Be strong; fear not! Behold, your God. . . will come and save you' " (Isaiah 35:4 ESV). And Psalm 60:12 (NLT) tells us, "With God's help we will do mighty things." The proof of such words is revealed in the lives and stories of the heroes of our faith. Consider Stephen's declaration about God's follower Joseph: "God was with him and rescued him out of all his afflictions and gave him favor and wisdom before Pharaoh, king of Egypt, who made him ruler over Egypt" (Acts 7:9–10 ESV).

The point is you need not give in to stress. Don't be afraid. Hand yourself and your circumstances over to God, knowing He'll save you, strengthen you, and help you do mighty things!

God, in You I can do mighty things!

YOUR BEST FRIEND

*"Now you are my friends, since I have told
you everything the Father told me."*
JOHN 15:15 NLT

If you're in a period of waiting, you need not stress. You are
not alone. Jesus is right there with you.

Jesus is your friend. He has promised never to leave you or
forsake you. During this time of waiting, Jesus is helping you to
grow, to discover, to learn, to prepare for the next step in your
life. And in the process, He is keeping you calm by leading you
to the words you need to read and hear, the promises you need
to embrace, to give you the strength to become the person you
were created to be. He asks you to "be sure of this: I am with
you always" (Matthew 28:20 NLT). Because that's what a good,
strong, and wise friend does. Sticks close to His little sister, the
burgeoning princess who is the apple of His eye.

*Thanks for waiting it out with me, Jesus, my Brother,
Savior, and Friend. Teach and tell me more!*

A WELL-WATERED TREE

"Blessed are those who trust in the LORD and have made the LORD their hope and confidence. They are like trees planted along a riverbank, with roots that reach deep into the water. Such trees are not bothered by the heat or worried by long months of drought."
JEREMIAH 17:7–8 NLT

God says that "those who put their trust in mere humans, who rely on human strength. . .are like stunted shrubs in the desert, with no hope for the future. They will live in the barren wilderness" (Jeremiah 17:5–6 NLT). But those who trust in Him, whose hope and confidence are in Him, are like trees by the water. Not only are they undisturbed by what happens in their environment, but "their leaves stay green, and they never stop producing fruit" (Jeremiah 17: 8 NLT).

You may not have the power to choose what happens to you, but you do have the power to change your attitude toward it. So trust in God, your hope and confidence in Him alone.

I'm making You my one and only hope, Lord.

FREE AND ENDLESS REFILLS

Ever be filled and stimulated with the [Holy] Spirit.
EPHESIANS 5:18 AMPC

In this world you can turn to many different things to fulfill yourself, to satisfy your cravings for energy, strength, even peace. But turning to the world's salve can lead to even more stress. God would have you turn to Him. Remember, being filled with Him and His Spirit is not a once and done thing, happening only when you profess your belief in Jesus. It's a continual refilling.

So turn to God. Recognize that "you are God's temple and that God's Spirit dwells in you" (1 Corinthians 3:16 ESV). Daily pray for God to refresh you deep within, taking into account that just as you likely "know how to give good gifts [gifts that are to their advantage] to your children, how much more will your heavenly Father give the Holy Spirit to those who ask and continue to ask Him!" (Luke 11:13 AMPC).

Lord, I am looking to be filled by You and Your Spirit. Refresh me now—over and over again!

TRUE REALITY

"GOD is with you, O mighty warrior!"
JUDGES 6:12 MSG

Gideon was trying to make the best of a stressful situation. The Midianites kept sending raiding parties into his territory. So Gideon was threshing wheat in his hiding place when an angel of God opened his eyes, calling him a "mighty warrior"! Gideon didn't feel that God was with him, nor that he, the least of his family, was anything but weak. But God again told him not to worry. That with God, Gideon was to "go with the strength you have, and rescue Israel from the Midianites" (Judges 6:14 NLT). Later, as Gideon did what God called him to do, "the Spirit of the LORD clothed Gideon with power" (Judges 6:34 NLT)—just when he needed it most.

Don't let your current situation stress you out. Know that God is with you and that you can move forward in the strength you have—because God will add His to it, just when you need it most.

Help me see the true reality I have with You in my life, Lord. Help me be Your mighty warrior!

Day 313

COME AWAY

*The apostles returned to Jesus and told him all that
they had done and taught. And he said to them, "Come
away by yourselves to a desolate place and rest a while."
For many were coming and going, and they had no
leisure even to eat. And they went away in the boat
to a desolate place by themselves.*

MARK 6:30–32 ESV

A bit stressed? Feel as if you don't even have time to eat? Jesus
knows exactly what you need.

First, go to Him and tell Him everything you have done.
Then follow the same advice He gave His other workers. Come
away. . .by yourself. . .to a quiet place. . .and rest awhile. It
doesn't have to be far away, just far enough to get away from
your "crowds." And you're to do it by yourself. Make sure the
place you're heading to is away from people, distractions, and
noise. Then, once you are there, take a deep breath. And "rest
a while," moving from de-stressed to blessed.

*I'm coming to meet with You, Lord.
I'm ready to rest in You.*

Day 314

LYING BACK

Unless the LORD builds a house, the work of the builders is wasted. . . . It is useless for you to work so hard from early morning until late at night, anxiously working for food to eat; for God gives rest to his loved ones.
PSALM 127:1–2 NLT

Yes, God wants you to work on the house that's being built. But He doesn't want you to be laboring from 4:00 a.m. to midnight (unless perhaps you're laboring to bring a new life into this world). He wants you to put some trust in Him, that He will use for good whatever you are putting your hand to.

So trust that God has a good purpose and outcome for all the work you are doing. Trust that He will always provide for you. Then get some rest, lying back in His arms, falling asleep with His breath warming your ear.

I'm ready to change up my schedule, Lord, to get more of the rest I so sorely need and You so readily give.

BELIEVE AND RECEIVE

Jesus met a man with an advanced case of leprosy. . . .
"Lord," he said, "if you are willing, you can heal me
and make me clean." Jesus reached out and touched
him. "I am willing," he said. "Be healed!"
And instantly the leprosy disappeared.
LUKE 5:12–13 NLT

God is willing to step into your situation and help you. He's willing to reach out His hand and touch you, commanding the problem to be solved, declaring you to be healed. Of this you must be certain. But to be touched by the loving hand of Jesus, you must meet up with Him. You must be as humble in His presence as was this leper who "bowed with his face to the ground" (Luke 5:12 NLT). You must not doubt but know that Jesus is willing, out of His love and compassion for you, to enter into your situation and sort out your problem. Jesus is willing to give—if you are willing to believe and receive.

Lord, shore up my faith. Help me be
willing to believe and receive!

PROTECTIVE WALL OF FIRE

The other angel said, "Hurry, and say to
that young man, 'Jerusalem will someday
be so full. . .there won't be room enough for
everyone! Many will live outside the city
walls. Then I, myself, will be a protective wall
of fire around Jerusalem, says the LORD. And I
will be the glory inside the city!' "
ZECHARIAH 2:3–5 NLT

Imagine, God being a protective wall of fire around you—*and*
the glory within you! Regarding verse 5, *John Gill's Exposition*
of the Entire Bible says, "The Targum [an ancient Aramaic
paraphrase or interpretation of the Hebrew Bible] paraphrases
it, 'my Word shall be unto her, saith the Lord, as a wall of fire
encompassing her round about.' "

When you feel stressed, remember God's protective wall of
fire. Reach out with your heart and mind and pull in a word
from God to keep the anxiety at bay, to feed the glory of His
presence within you, to generate the calming warmth His Word
alone can give.

Lord, I feel Your wall of fire protecting me!
May Your glory within keep stress without!

THE WAY TO TURN

*When I am overwhelmed, you alone know the way
I should turn. . . . Then I pray to you, O Lord.
I say, "You are my place of refuge. You are all I
really want in life. . . . Bring me out of prison so
I can thank you. . .for you are good to me."*
Psalm 142:3, 5, 7 nlt

Even if stress causes us to lose direction, God will know the
way we should go, the next steps we should take. But we need
to reach out and tell Him where we are. It's not that He doesn't
know. It's that we need to recognize, have an awareness of, the
place we find ourselves in. Praying to Him will help us reaffirm
our priorities, state the true reality of our situation.

In God, we have a place to run. He's all we need. In His
power and strength, He'll "bring us out."

*When I'm losing my way, You know my
next steps. So I'm praying to You, Lord.
Shower me with Your goodness!*

PRESENCE AND POWER

The Lord brought us forth out of Egypt with
a mighty hand and with an outstretched arm,
and with great (awesome) power and
with signs and with wonders.
DEUTERONOMY 26:8 AMPC

Never doubt that God can get you out of a stressful situation.
He did it over and over again for His people—and will do it
over and over again for you. That is, of course, unless He wants
you to learn something while you're in your specific situation,
as He wanted the Israelites to trust in His promise to lead them
into the land of milk and honey instead of focusing on the
false reality of giants in that land. The point is to refrain from
worry. Don't stress or be anxious. Remain in His power and
love. Know that God is with you no matter what you're going
through. And that, when He's ready, He'll bring you out with
a mighty hand in an amazing way.

Thank You, Lord, for Your presence
and power in my life.

Day 319

BEFORE, BEHIND, AND BESIDE

You go before me and follow me.
You place your hand of blessing on my head.
PSALM 139:5 NLT

No matter what your worries are, you never face anything alone. God has gone before you and seen what's ahead. He'll be following behind you to protect you from the rear. And He's right here beside you, with His hand of blessing upon your head.

Keep these truths in the forefront of your mind and you'll see there's no reason to fret. God has everything under control—according to His plan, His timing, His ideas for you. So relax into all that's happening. Keep alert for the voice of the Spirit, telling you which way to go. Follow without fear, for you have the strongest being in the world—the God of the universe—before, behind, and beside you. You are blessed.

Lord, help me constantly keep the reality of Your
presence with me in my heart, mind, body,
soul, and spirit. For I know with You a
breath away, I have nothing to fear.

EVERLASTING LIGHT

If I ride the wings of the morning, if I dwell by the farthest oceans, even there your hand will guide me, and your strength will support me. . . . How precious are your thoughts about me, O God. They cannot be numbered! . . . And when I wake up, you are still with me!

PSALM 139:9–10, 17–18 NLT

No matter how deep you get sucked under, no matter how long you stay in the stress zone, God will find you, will pull you back out, guide you with His wisdom, support you with His strength. You are on His mind, under His watchful eye night and day.

You may never be as dedicated to Him as He is to you. But you can take steps to get closer to Him by spending time in His presence and digging into His Word. Then ask Him to search your heart, to know your "anxious thoughts," to "point out anything" in you that offends Him, and to lead you "along the path of everlasting life" (verses 23–24 NLT).

You know all about me, Lord.
Help me to know Your path for me.

BOLD AS A LION

"Fear not, stand firm, and see the salvation of the LORD,
which he will work for you today. For the Egyptians
whom you see today, you shall never see again. The
LORD will fight for you, and you have only to be silent."
EXODUS 14:13–14 ESV

The Israelites had the Red Sea in front of them and Pharaoh's army behind them. It looked like there was no way out. But God had a plan. He told Moses, "Lift up your staff, and stretch out your hand over the sea and divide it, that the people of Israel may go through the sea on dry ground" (verses 15–16 ESV).

With walls of water on both sides of them, that's just what the Israelites did. "Bold as lions" (Proverbs 28:1 NLT), they walked through the seabed and gained the other side before the Egyptians could touch one stitch of their clothing.

Never feel trapped. Be bold as a lion. And watch the Lord fight for you!

With You in my life, Lord, I need not fear.
Help me stand firm in You.

LABELS

*Jabez was a better man than his brothers, a man of
honor. . . . Jabez prayed to the God of Israel: "Bless
me, O bless me! Give me land, large tracts of land.
And provide your personal protection—don't let evil
hurt me." God gave him what he asked.*
1 CHRONICLES 4:9–10 MSG

Each one of us bears a label, whether it's given to us by our
parents, peers, siblings, friends, or even ourselves. Our label
might be skinny, chunky, weakling, cheat, addict, money-
grabber, shark, poor, failure, etc. But life is stressful enough
without wearing a badge of dishonor.

Jabez had a label. Having had a difficult labor, his mom
named him "pain." But Jabez refused to see himself that way,
to go through life with that misnomer. So he prayed with all
his heart to God, asking Him to bless his life, give him more
responsibility, and protect him. God granted his request.

What label do you need to leave at God's feet?

*Lord, remove this label. Help me see myself with
Your eyes—blessed, responsible, and protected.*

Day 323
HOW TO PREVAIL

They were given help against them, and the Hagrites
or Ishmaelites were delivered into their hands, and
all who were allied with them, for they cried to
God in the battle; and He granted their entreaty,
because they relied on, clung to, and trusted in Him.
1 CHRONICLES 5:20 AMPC

Descendants of Reuben, Gad, and Manasseh, men described as "valiant" and "skillful in war" (verse 18 AMPC), went to war against the Hagrites and their allies. But during the battle, things must not have been going so well because the Israelites "cried to God." And He helped them prevail! Why? Because they "relied on, clung to, and trusted in" their God.

What battle are you waging? Have you cried out to God for help, or are you stressed out because you're trying to win the day in your own strength? Rely on God, cling to Him, know He is your Savior. And He will help you prevail.

I'm crying to You, Lord, trusting
in You with all I am!

BREAKING THE SILENCE

The LORD detests the sacrifice of the wicked,
but he delights in the prayers of the upright.
PROVERBS 15:8 NLT

Sometimes we get so immersed in the happenings of this physical life that we forget to look up, to catch our breath, to spend time with the One who can lift us above all the stress and uncertainty that's weighing us down. We forget we have a God who loves to spend time with us. A God who delights in our prayers. A God who's leaning down, bending His ear to our lips, yearning for us to utter one little sound. He wants to help, guide, forgive, hold, carry, provide for, and love.

Know that God finds joy in your presence and is eager to listen to anything you have to say. So rant, rave, love, crave, plead, beg, or just babble about your day. But go to the One who longs to hear your voice. Break the silence. Pray.

Lord, thank You for being such a wonderful
God and friend. Let's talk.

EXPECTATIONS

*Love GOD, all you saints; GOD takes care of all who stay
close to him. . . . Be brave. Be strong. Don't give up.
Expect GOD to get here soon.*

PSALM 31:23–24 MSG

It's important to evaluate your expectations. Are you hoping
other people will give you some sort of break? That money will
fall from the sky? That circumstances you can't control will
miraculously change in your favor? Or are you sticking close
to God, hoping in Him, expecting Him to take charge not just
of your situation, but of you—mind, body, spirit, and soul?

No matter what's happening in your life, keep praying. Be
like the psalmist who tells God: "Desperate, I throw myself on
you: you are my God! Hour by hour I place my days in your
hand" (Psalm 31:14–15 MSG). Then stay brave and strong,
waiting for, hoping for, and expecting God to step into your
midst any moment.

*I'm never giving up, Lord. I'm sticking with You,
knowing You'll get me through.*

RELAX

How do you know what your life will be like tomorrow? Your life is like the morning fog—it's here a little while, then it's gone. What you ought to say is, "If the Lord wants us to, we will live and do this or that."

JAMES 4:14–15 NLT

We're women. Upon awakening, we usually have a mental plan around what we'll wear, what work needs to get done, what meals we're going to cook, what pick-ups and drop-offs are required, and what pleasures we may be able to partake in before bed. But then something happens. We get interrupted by an unplanned event, circumstance, or obligation. And yet we still try to work out our day according to our schedule, holding on to our original plan with a white-knuckled grip, causing stress within and without.

No more! Relax. Allow some things to fall by the wayside. Take the attitude that "if the Lord wants us to, we will live and do this or that." And let the chips fall where they may.

My day is in Your hands, Lord. Now I can relax!

HIS ONCE AGAIN

*The LORD your God is in your midst. . .he will rejoice
over you with gladness; he will quiet you by his love;
he will exult over you with loud singing.*
ZEPHANIAH 3:17 ESV

Feeling alone? As if the world is on your shoulders, weighing
you down? As if you can't take one more day of this stress?
Step back and give a shrug, allowing the world to roll off your
shoulders. Then look right in front of you. There is God. He
is right there with you, living, working, playing by your side.
He is grinning from ear to ear, so glad He is that you are with
Him. He's going to soothe you with His great love, going to rid
you of all the things you fear. And once that balm is applied,
once the stress is no longer clouding your vision and stopping
up your ears, He's going to celebrate by singing over you.

Step back. Look straight ahead. "God is in your midst."
Listen to His song!

*Sing to me, Lord. Love me; ease my mind
and heart. Make me Yours once again.*

MIGHTY WIND

When the enemy shall come in like a flood, the Spirit of the Lord will. . .put him to flight [for He will come like a rushing stream which the breath of the Lord drives].
ISAIAH 59:19 AMPC

No matter how much stress tries to drown you, a greater force is ready to come in "like a rushing stream." A force no power can withstand: the Spirit of the Lord. He's a mighty wind, ready to blow you out of whatever dark waters you may be in.

Your only job is to walk close to Him; to obey His command to love Him with all you are and love others as yourself; and, of course, to pray. You can't have any kind of relationship with anyone—either your Father in heaven or others on earth—unless you have open lines of communication, lines through which you speak *and* listen.

Know God is here for you. Trust Him to blow any negatives, bad attitudes, and stressors out of your waters. Pray for His breath to deliver you now.

Lord, put my negative thoughts to flight.
Then flood me with Your never-ending love.

TRUTH

*Jesus said, "I am the Road, also the Truth, also the Life.
No one gets to the Father apart from me. If you really
knew me, you would know my Father as well. From
now on, you do know him. You've even seen him!"*

JOHN 14:6–7 MSG

In this world of "fake news" where we are surrounded by loads of misinformation, it's wonderfully reassuring to delve into the truth of God's Word written thousands of years ago, wisdom that has stood the test of time. How comforting and amazing that we have access to and can follow the Word that reveals God the Father to us, helping us to know Him and what He would have us do.

Keep the truth, wisdom, and knowledge the Bible provides close to your heart. Write it on the walls of your mind. Cling to it amid trials and you'll find a peace that surpasses all understanding. Stay on the Road, stick to the Truth, and you'll be living the life God has planned for you and those you love.

You, Lord, are my Truth.

GOD ALONE

*For God alone, O my soul, wait in silence,
for my hope is from him. He only is my rock
and my salvation, my fortress; I shall not be
shaken. . . . Trust in him at all times. . .pour
out your heart before him; God is a refuge for us.*
PSALM 62:5–6, 8 ESV

When stress comes knocking at your door, remember to breathe. Then calm your heart by reminding your soul to wait in silence. Know that your hope is in God alone. He's the firm foundation you can stand tall on, the solid Rock, the Unchanging One. He's the One who saves you—over and over again. He's the One you can run to, the One who is always there for you.

Because God is in your life, nothing can shake you up. So breathe. Then pour out your heart to the One you trust. The One who protects you, who is your ultimate shelter in the storm *and* in the sun. He's waiting.

*Here's my heart, Lord. I come to You for peace,
for assurance, for help, for sanctuary, for love.*

GOD'S GOODNESS

*No doubt about it! God is good—good
to good people, good to the good-hearted.
But I nearly missed it, missed seeing his
goodness. I was looking the other way.*
PSALM 73:1–3 MSG

Sometimes, when our eyes drift away from God, we find them settling onto people who seem to have made it further than we have. Ones who, although they are less than godly, seem to be blessed. We then wonder what we have to do, how much harder we have to work, to have the "good life." And become stressed out trying to make it in this world.

This is when we need to turn our eyes to Jesus, realizing that those who are living without Him will "never be heard from again" (verse 27 MSG). Nevertheless, we may say, "But I'm in the very presence of God—oh, how refreshing it is! I've made Lord GOD my home" (verse 28 MSG).

*I know it's good for me to be near You, Lord.
You are my refuge, my life, my heart, my all.*

BRIMMING OVER

*Oh! May the God of green hope fill you up with joy,
fill you up with peace, so that your believing lives,
filled with the life-giving energy of the Holy Spirit,
will brim over with hope!*

ROMANS 15:13 MSG

Having hope can be a major de-stressor. It's about putting your worries aside and focusing on what *could* be. That doesn't mean you take a dreamy stance, just wondering what will happen next while you wait on the sidelines. It involves your taking some kind of action, giving all you can, doing all you can, to make that hope a reality. Yet at the same time, you're to put the entire situation, person, problem, or issue into God's hands. For in *Him* is your true hope. No matter what happens, you trust in the One who has your best interests at heart, the One who knows all, who sees beyond what you see, who will do what is best for His world, His people, His planet.

My hope is in You, Lord! I'm brimming over!

LIFT

The Lord is my Strength and my [impenetrable] Shield;
my heart trusts in, relies on, and confidently leans
on Him, and I am helped; therefore my heart greatly
rejoices, and with my song will I praise Him. . . .
Save Your people. . .nourish and shepherd
them and carry them forever.
PSALM 28:7, 9 AMPC

When we have nothing left within us—no energy, no strength, no light—we must reach out, cry out to the One who has all the answers, who can hold us safely in His arms until we are able to rise again and carry on—for Him.

So lift your arms toward heaven. Call on your Rock, Refuge, and Fortress. Allow His power to flow into you as you rest quietly, calmly in His arms. Trust Him to handle all you cannot, to work out those situations in which you see no way out. Allow Him to be your strength. Then sing your song of praise as He brings you back into the light.

I lift my eyes and arms to You, Lord.

PRECIOUS

*When you pass through the waters, I will be
with you; and through the rivers, they shall not
overwhelm you; when you walk through fire
you shall not be burned, and the flame shall
not consume you. For I am the Lord your
God. . . . You are precious in my eyes. . . .
Fear not, for I am with you.*

Isaiah 43:2–5 esv

When you're stressed, you feel as if you're walking alone. As if no
one knows what you're really going through or sees how much
you're suffering. You feel as if you're drowning in a flood and
no one hears your cries. Having been burned so many times,
you feel as if you're walking through fire. You wonder who, if
anyone, can save you.

Then you hear a voice, feel a touch, sense a presence. You
taste something good. It's the Holy Spirit reaching out for you,
walking right beside you, strong and mighty to save. God is
with you, and you are precious in His eyes. Impress this truth
upon your mind.

I will not fear, Lord, for You are beside me.

A NEW WAY

*Thus says the Lord, Who makes a way through the sea
and a path through the mighty waters. . . . Do not
[earnestly] remember the former things; neither consider
the things of old. Behold, I am doing a new thing! Now
it springs forth; do you not perceive and know it and
will you not give heed to it? I will even make a way in
the wilderness and rivers in the desert.*

ISAIAH 43:16, 18–19 AMPC

You have chosen to walk a new road. To trust the One who
makes a way where you can see no way, the One who has forgiven and forgotten all the mistakes you've made.

So put your hand in the hand of the One who is ready to
do a new thing in your life. Forget what has passed. Look to
God in confidence, knowing He has already cleared a path for
you, the precious daughter He has called by name (see Isaiah
43:1). Answer His call and walk forward in His presence.

Lord, thank You for being my peace and my life.

CULTIVATING CALM

*I've cultivated a quiet heart. Like a baby content
in its mother's arms, my soul is a baby content.*
PSALM 131:2 MSG

Psalm 131 was written by King David, who trained himself to trust God, to put all things in His hands. David saw God as a stable, ever-present, and powerful force for good and right in his life.

That's why David could say, "My soul waits calmly for God alone" (Psalm 62:1 GW). He looked for no other outside influence—no people, strong horses, tools, weapons, or money—to rescue him. To firm that up within himself, he'd talk to his soul: "Wait calmly for God alone, my soul, because my hope comes from him. He alone is my rock and my savior—my stronghold. I cannot be shaken" (Psalm 62:5–6 GW).

You too can cultivate a quiet heart and calm soul by making God your sole rock and stronghold. Pray to Him and remind yourself that He alone can—and will—handle everything that comes your way.

*You alone, Lord, are my Savior. Be calm,
my soul. Be content, my heart.*

A STUDENT OF PRAYER

Then He was praying in a certain place; and when He stopped, one of His disciples said to Him, Lord, teach us to pray. . . . And He said to them, When you pray, say: Our Father Who is in heaven, hallowed be Your name.

LUKE 11:1–2 AMPC

The disciples had witnessed the power, joy, and wisdom Jesus exuded in their presence. They'd also seen Him go off alone to pray. So one asked Him, "Lord, teach us to pray."

Through the example of Jesus and His disciples, it's clear that prayer is the antidote to worry. The stronger you are in prayer, the less your concerns will weigh you down.

Today, come to Jesus as a willing and worthy student. Ask Him to teach you how to weaken your worries and build up your faith as you learn to pray with power. Start with the basics. Pray this "Disciples' Prayer" (see Luke 11:2–4), knowing Abba God is longing to hear what you have to say.

Abba God, hear my prayer. "Our Father Who is in heaven. . ."

GIVING GOD THE DETAILS

Hezekiah took the letters from the messengers,
read them, and went to the LORD's temple.
He spread them out in front of the LORD
and prayed to the LORD.
2 KINGS 19:14–15 GW

Hezekiah was the king of Judah. Here we find he's received letters filled with threats of attack from Sennacherib of Assyria. After reading them, Hezekiah didn't panic but went to the temple of the Lord. There he spread out the threatening messages before the Lord and prayed, acknowledging God as the supreme Ruler and Creator of heaven and earth. He asked God to listen to him, to open His ears and hear Sennacherib's message, and to come to the rescue of His people. And God did.

When you have a massive problem, don't panic. Go to God, and then lay all the details before Him. Ask Him to save you. And He will.

Lord of all, here's what's happening. . . .
I'm resolved not to panic but come to
You for in You alone will I find help.

THE ONE WHO COMFORTS

"I, yes I, am the one who comforts you.
So why are you afraid of mere humans,
who wither like the grass and disappear?"
ISAIAH 51:12 NLT

God understands you like no other. He knows your worries, fears, hopes, dreams, and passions. He sees what's going on in your life. That's why Father God wants to fill you, His daughter, with assurance that He alone is the One who can and does comfort you. He is all-powerful and eternal, unlike humans, who'll one day fade away, wither like the grass, and become as nothing.

So when you are worried or fearful about what some person might say or do next, draw close to the "one who comforts you" like no other. Lean into God, His power, promises, and protection. Remind yourself of who He is and the solace He and His presence provide. Allow His love and light to pour over you as you pray.

Abba God, pour Your love, light, and protection
over me. In You I find the comfort that
melts all fears and worries.

INSIDE THE CIRCLE OF PROTECTION

*GOD met me more than halfway, he freed me from my
anxious fears. . . . When I was desperate, I called out,
and GOD got me out of a tight spot. GOD's angel sets
up a circle of protection around us while we pray.*
PSALM 34:4, 6–7 MSG

When you're weighed down by anxiety, God is ready to meet
you "more than halfway." All you need to do is cry out to Him;
tell Him everything that's on your mind, all your fears, worries,
and troubles. "Never hide your feelings from him" (Psalm 34:5
MSG). Although God knows what you're fearing and worrying
about and all the troubles in your midst, He wants you to
voice them, to unload them upon Him, to get them out of
your system.

Once you do, God will rescue you and fill you with His
peace; His angel will set up a protective circle around you until you are able to rise up again in strength. Don't neglect the
privilege and benefit of prayer. It's a life saver.

Here's what's happening, Lord. . . . Save me!

THE FATHER WHO LISTENS

*I love the LORD because he hears my voice and my
prayer for mercy. Because he bends down to listen,
I will pray as long as I have breath!*
PSALM 116:1–2 NLT

Listening has almost become a lost art among humans. But
there's one person who will *always* pay attention to what you
have to say: God—a supernatural, all-powerful Father who
actually *bends down to listen* to what you, His daughter, is
saying!

Fix firmly in your mind that image of God bending down
to you. See yourself as the woman-child that so desperately
needs her Father to hear all her woes and worries. Why like
a child? Because "the LORD protects those of childlike faith"
(Psalm 116:6 NLT).

When you put all your trust in Father God, when you
tell Him that you believe in Him and are deeply troubled (see
Psalm 116:10), you'll come away free from fretting, and your
soul will "be at rest again" (Psalm 116:7 NLT).

*Lord, I want the soul-rest only You
can supply. Listen. . .*

OUT OF SELF AND INTO JESUS

Jesus. . .said to them, If anyone intends to come after Me, let him deny himself [forget, ignore, disown, and lose sight of himself and his own interests] and take up his cross, and . . .follow with Me [continually, cleaving steadfastly to Me].

MARK 8:34 AMPC

Some worries are egocentric. You worry you won't be promoted, you won't get the house you bid on, you'll never get ahead monetarily, and so on. In this land of worry, it's all about you. But Jesus wants you to realize it's really all about Him and that if you want to be His follower, you're to lose sight of yourself and your own interests.

That's a tall order, but it is possible and so much more freeing than fretting. When you empty yourself of your concerns, you have more room to hold what God wants to give you.

Get out of yourself and into Jesus. You'll find you won't regret it.

Jesus, help me focus on You alone. I want to get out of myself and into You!

EXPECT THE UNEXPECTED

*Seeing Peter and John about to go into the temple, he asked
to receive alms. And Peter directed his gaze at him, as did
John, and said, "Look at us." And he fixed his attention on
them, expecting to receive something from them.*
ACTS 3:3–5 ESV

When you bring your worries to God, chances are you also let
Him know how you'd like things worked out before you leave
them all in His hands. In other words, you let God know what
you expect to happen. But sometimes what you think you expect
is not the best thing for you.

Take the lame man sitting outside the temple. He expected
Peter and John to give him money. But they gave him something
else—healing in Jesus' name!

Rest assured that when you hand your troubles over to God,
He'll go deeper, to the very core of your desire, and discover
what you really want. Expect God to give you the unexpected,
the better thing.

*Lord, when I give You my concerns,
help me expect the unexpected!*

Day 344

POWER AND PEACE ARE YOURS

The LORD will give power to his people.
The LORD will bless his people with peace.
PSALM 29:11 GW

The statements above are so simple. Yet they're filled with power.

God is ruler over all. And you're His daughter, one of "his people." Thus, on days when you're weakened by worry, you can go to God for all the strength you need. He'll give you the power to persevere and prevail. And, good daughter, He'll also bless you with peace in this very moment and all the moments to come.

There's only one caveat. You need to *believe*, to fix these facts firmly in your mind so you'll not feel helpless and veer from the path He's laid out for you.

So drop your worries by the doorstep as you enter God's presence. Take in all the strength and peace, which He's *always* waiting to give you. And go on your way in His name and power.

Lord, my God and King, I come into Your
presence. Fill me with Your power and
peace so I may do Your will.

GETTING IN HARMONY WITH GOD

"Be in harmony and at peace with God. In this way you will have prosperity. Accept instruction from his mouth, and keep his words in your heart."

JOB 22:21–22 GW

When you're caught up in a cycle of worry and anxiety, you're not in harmony with God. On top of that, your fretting begins to become a barrier between you and Him. This keeps you from receiving the full power, strength, and peace God aches to give you.

Today, get back in harmony with God. Put your trust in the words and promises of the love letter (the Bible) He's written just for you. Ingest His wisdom and follow it, allowing it to have full sway over your thoughts. Don't just *write* His words on your heart; *keep* them there so when worry flares up, you can quench it with God's wisdom. In so doing, you'll find yourself prospering more than you ever dreamed or imagined.

I want Your song in my heart, Lord. Help me leave my worry behind as I get myself back in harmony with You.

GOD IS NEAR

The LORD is close to the brokenhearted;
he rescues those whose spirits are crushed.
PSALM 34:18 NLT

Human beings are fragile creatures. As one such being, your heart can break, your spirit be crushed. It can happen after hearing mean words from someone or suffering the betrayal of someone you counted on and trusted. Maybe it happened upon the death of a loved one. Perhaps it was the loss of a job, a house, a business, a pastor, a friend. Whatever the cause, upon the heels of a broken heart and a crushed spirit, anxiety is sure to follow. You wonder, *Why did it happen? How do I go on from here?*

Know that in the midst of trial, God is right there with you. He's holding you in His arms. He'll heal your heart, restore your spirit, and alleviate your anxiety. You need say nothing more than, "Lord. . .help me."

Thank You, Lord, for always being there when I need You.
You're the one sure thing I can count on. You will heal
my heart, revive my spirit, and calm my soul.

YOUR HIDING PLACE

For you are my hiding place; you protect me from
trouble. You surround me with songs of victory.
PSALM 32:7 NLT

Physically, it's difficult to find a place where you can truly hide. Someone will always find you, whether it be the kids, the boss, the husband, or the boyfriend. It's almost as if their radar goes off whenever you want to find a moment alone.

Yet spiritually there is one place you can always go to get away from all people and all worry. It's in God's presence. Once you're there, you find yourself surrounded with not just love and encouragement but with songs of victory.

God is your biggest cheerleader and best coach. He says, "I will guide you along the best pathway for your life. I will advise you and watch over you" (Psalm 32:8 NLT). His only caveat is for you not to be stubborn when He tells you which way to go, what to do. But that's a small price to pay to live in victory.

Lord, I come to hide in You. Save me, guide me.
Make me putty in Your hands.

BLESSINGS TO GOD'S BELOVED

Except the Lord builds the house, they labor in vain
who build it. . . . It is vain for you to rise up early, to
take rest late, to eat the bread of [anxious] toil—for He
gives [blessings] to His beloved in sleep.
Psalm 127:1–2 ampc

God wants His daughters to be useful. But without God's blessing on your work or ministry, not only will all your efforts be useless, but you will find yourself exhausted, eating the "bread of [anxious] toil," "work[ing] your worried fingers to the bone" (Psalm 127:2 msg).

To live and work a worry-free life, ask God how He'd like you to use the gifts with which you've been blessed. Then follow where He leads, taking on the job or ministry He's directing you toward.

Once you're in the space God has provided, invite Him into every moment of your workday. Put your efforts and their outcome in His hands. Then you'll have the peace and rest God is so willing and able to give those He loves.

I'm resting in You, Lord, my provider, my love.

NOT KNOWING

We have no might to stand against this great company
that is coming against us. We do not know
what to do, but our eyes are upon You.
2 CHRONICLES 20:12 AMPC

God is thrilled when we are humble, when we admit we have
no idea what to do but are looking to Him for help, wisdom,
guidance, and direction. At the same time, admitting to ourselves
that we don't know what to do takes all the pressure off us! In
fact, much of our strength lies in believing God. What a relief
that we don't need to have all the answers! How wonderful to
admit—even to our spouses, children, and friends, if we must—
that we don't know what to do next but are looking to God.

Know that God will always come through, no matter how
bad things may look. He'll take care of all that's coming against
you. He'll bring you out of whatever crisis you find yourself in.

Thank You, God, that I don't need to have all
the answers—because You have them for me!

LOOK UP

*I press on to reach the end of the race and
receive the heavenly prize for which God,
through Christ Jesus, is calling us.*
PHILIPPIANS 3:14 NLT

God has given us a vision for our lives. We are reaching for the
prize that is awaiting us, that to which Jesus is calling us. We
have something to strive for.

Thus we need not get caught up in the cycle of bad news.
We need not lose hope. We can choose to see God before us,
feel Jesus' warm breath upon us, hear the Spirit's voice within
us, giving us guidance, telling us to keep our cool.

Have your eyes been glued to the ground? Are you dragging
your feet? Is your chin on your chest? Look up to what God
is doing. Keep your eyes on His heavenly prize. Know that
God has a purpose for your life and that He will brighten up
whatever darkness may come your way.

*My eyes are on You, Jesus. I'm walking in Your light,
feeling Your breath, hearing Your voice.*

THE UPSIDE

When troubles of any kind come your way,
consider it an opportunity for great joy.
JAMES 1:2 NLT

We all sometimes find ourselves going through dark days, groping for a way out. But there is an upside to these times: When we are tested, we come out better and stronger than before.

Consider the Old Testament hero Joseph who was thrown into a pit, sold to traders, and imprisoned unjustly. Yet he went on to become the number two man in Egypt. Why? Because no matter what happened to him, no matter where he landed, he had faith that "the Lord was with him and made whatever he did to prosper" (Genesis 39:23 AMPC; see also 39:2)!

Even though you might not be where you'd like to be, don't stress about it. Just have faith. Know that God is with you. He's building up your resilience, bringing out the best in you, training you up for the next steps as He prospers you right where you are.

Lord, help me to find joy wherever I land,
knowing You're there, helping me not
just to survive but to thrive!

CHOICES

Then Jehoshaphat said to the king of Israel, "But first, find out what the LORD's word is in this matter."
1 Kings 22:5 GW

King Ahab wanted to try to reclaim some territory. But Jehoshaphat, king of Judah, wasn't taking one step until he asked the Lord's advice.

When we make choices without first consulting the Lord—or even worse, when we do things against His advice—we can end up not only feeling stressed out but facing ruin. So for less stress in your life, be like the wise Jehoshaphat. Seek God's advice *before* you choose. Pray, "Make your ways known to me, O LORD, and teach me your paths. Lead me in your truth and teach me because you are God, my savior. I wait all day long for you" (Psalm 25:4–5 GW).

Know that God will give you all the wisdom you need for where you are and will keep you from tripping up on your path (see Psalm 25:14–15).

Give me light for my path, Lord. I'm not moving until You speak.

FOLLOW HIM

*And rising very early in the morning, while it
was still dark, he departed and went out to a
desolate place, and there he prayed.*

MARK 1:35 ESV

Jesus was up against a lot of different political and religious factions. He was pressed by the crowds that were seeking healing physically, emotionally, mentally, and spiritually. He was teaching and training disciples who just didn't seem to get it right. He was pressured by Satan who was trying to tempt Him away from His mission. He encountered people in His own hometown—even family members—who either didn't believe Him or wanted Him to tip His hand before it was time.

Yet in spite of all the things He was up against, Jesus never panicked but kept His peace. How? He went off alone and sought His Father God. He left the crowds and went to a deserted and desolate place. Somewhere secluded where He could meet with God one-on-one in the quiet of the morning hours.

Follow Him.

Lord, I come to You now, alone, seeking Your face.

SEEKING APPROVAL

I'm not trying to win the approval of people,
but of God. If pleasing people were my goal,
I would not be Christ's servant.

GALATIANS 1:10 NLT

Abraham Lincoln said, "You can please some of the people all of the time, you can please all of the people some of the time, but you can't please all of the people all of the time." Yet that is exactly what we sometimes try to do. And in the process, we end up getting stressed out, because pleasing everyone is an unattainable goal. We are looking for love and approval in all the wrong places. But what's a girl to do?

Look for *God's* approval only. Don't worry what other people might say or do. It's Him you're looking to please. It's in Him you feel secure. It's He who loves you beyond measure, who has created you for a specific reason. So make Him number one in your life, seeking to live for Him alone.

I hope to please You, Lord, in all I say,
think, and do. Show me how to serve You!

TRUST AND PRAY

Trust God from the bottom of your heart; don't try to figure out everything on your own. Listen for God's voice in everything you do, everywhere you go; he's the one who will keep you on track.
PROVERBS 3:5–6 MSG

One surefire way to keep a lot of stress out of your life is to trust God. Do so from the very core of your being—mentally, physically, emotionally, and spiritually. Believe His promises, that He means all things for your good. That He loves you more than any other person you know. That He has a plan for your life. That He has got not only your back but your front.

Don't depend on yourself and your own finite ideas. Instead, depend on the One who is part of infinity itself, who sees a way beyond current appearances and impressions. Who knows your future—and your past.

Pray. Tell God what's happening. Ask Him to speak. Then actually listen to what He says. Do what He tells you to do. Pray more, stress less.

Lord, here I am. Tell me what to do.

KEEP CALM

"When reports come in of wars and rumored wars, keep your head and don't panic. This is routine history; this is no sign of the end."
MATTHEW 24:6 MSG

These days, just listening to the news can be a major stressor. For you hear of wars not only between nations but within nations. Then there are the wars on drugs, sex trafficking, opioid addiction, and so on. It's enough to discourage and dishearten even the most stoic of listeners.

Yet Jesus tells you not to panic. To keep your head. That this is just how it is. Meanwhile, what are you to do to keep calm and carry on?

One solution is to limit your exposure to the news. Find a level you can tolerate and maintain it. Another is to pray for all those involved in wars. Above all, replace those world worries with God's wisdom. Pray and memorize Bible verses to help you stay above the fray. Here's one to start you off:

You will keep in perfect peace all who trust in you, all whose thoughts are fixed on you! (Isaiah 26:3 NLT).

JESUS ON BOARD

Then they were quite willing and glad for Him to come into the boat. And now the boat went at once to the land they had steered toward.
JOHN 6:21 AMPC

Jesus having gone off to a mountain to pray, His disciples decided to head home across the sea. So they got into a boat and started rowing. As the darkness increased, Jesus was still a no-show. Meanwhile, the going got tough as a violent wind whipped up the waves. After straining against the oars for three or four miles, the disciples suddenly saw someone walking on the water near them. Their imaginations went wild and they became terrified. Jesus then calmed their fears, saying, "It is I; be not afraid!" (verse 20 AMPC).

When you're straining at the oars, be courageous and keep your eyes open for Jesus. When you see Him, invite Him to come aboard. Before you know it, you'll find yourself attaining that for which you were striving.

O mighty Navigator of my life, bring me toward the shore for which I strive!

Day 358
GOING BACK

"Go back the way you came through the desert."
1 KINGS 19:15 MSG

God directs Elijah to go back the way he'd come, which would put less and less distance between himself and the threats of Jezebel, the evil queen (and wife of King Ahab of Israel) he'd just run away from. Then, once he got there, Elijah's orders were, among other things, to anoint Jehu to be the new king over Israel!

Sooner or later, we will face circumstances in which we feel threatened. When we give in to our flesh, we may run away in fear and despair, only to find later that, having rediscovered God and heard His instructions, we *have* to go back and deal with the situation. That's when we must focus on the fact that God has the upper hand in any situation we find ourselves facing, that He will provide for us while we are back in the desert, and that He will help us find the courage to confront what frightened us in the first place.

I'm focused on Your power, Lord.
Help me face whatever lies ahead.

Day 359
OUR AVENUE

"Let not your hearts be troubled. Believe in God; believe also in me. . . . Peace I leave with you; my peace I give to you. Not as the world gives do I give to you. Let not your hearts be troubled, neither let them be afraid."
JOHN 14:1, 27 ESV

Stress is nothing to be ashamed of. It's just a signal to be recognized and addressed. The problem is when we let stress take over, try to ignore it, or imagine we can handle it in our own strength.

God knew we'd have trouble in this life, that we'd find ourselves with anxiety-causing stress. But He also gave us a way out: Jesus. Our faith in Him is our avenue to an out-of-this-world peace.

Jesus is waiting. Take a deep belly breath. Exhale. Enter that secret place where He abides. Ask Him to cover you with His wings, to raise you up. To give you the word you need to hear, the peace you need to inhale.

I'm here, Lord, limp in Your arms.
Please fill me with Your peace.

A HEART FOR HEARING

*A quiet voice asked, "So Elijah, now tell me,
what are you doing here?"*
1 Kings 19:13 msg

Not happy with Elijah's initial version of events, God tells him
to come out of his cave and stand on the mountain. A strong
wind comes by, breaking up the rocks. But God isn't in the
wind. Then an earthquake—but still no God. Then a fire—but
still no God. After the fire, in the silence that remains, comes
a gentle voice. A whisper. *That's* when Elijah comes out of the
cave, still *hiding* from God, masking his face with his cloak. As
Elijah stands there, God asks him again, "What are you doing
here?" And Elijah repeats his tale of woe and desperation.

God asks you to have a heart for His message. To stand
before Him with *boldness*. To calmly listen. When you do, you
will hear His still, small voice in the silence of your days.

*Lord, help me to have a heart for Your
message as I boldly come before You,
calmly listening for Your whisper.*

HIS STORY

What are you doing here?
1 KINGS 19:9 AMPC

On Horeb, the mount of God, Elijah reaches a cave and sets up camp. There God asks—not once, but twice—"What are you doing here?" In response, Elijah tells God—not once, but twice—his story. How he's been fighting for God. But the Israelites don't seem to care. Other prophets have been murdered and the people are now looking to kill him, the only one of God's prophets left!

Yet God knows the true story, *His* story. He knows more prophets are left (see 1 Kings 18:4). That Jezebel is the only one who has threatened him. That Elijah seems to have forgotten His previous mighty acts.

When we replace God's story with our own, nothing but despair echoes in our heads. That's because our feelings have usurped God's truth. The story in our mind has overtaken *His* story for our lives. That's when we know it's time to change the thoughts in our head and get back to the true story.

Lord, help me zero in on Your story for my life.

STRENGTH FOR THE JOURNEY

"Arise and eat, for the journey is too great for you."
1 KINGS 19:7 ESV

Even God's most faithful can find themselves stressed out. Consider Elijah. After his victory with God, Elijah received a threatening message from Jezebel. Yet instead of waiting for a word from God, this prophet ran for his life. Over eighty miles later, Elijah sat down under a broom tree, asked God to take his life, and fell asleep.

God responded by sending Elijah an angel who touched him, said, "Arise and eat," and provided him with bread and water, giving Elijah enough strength for his next steps.

When you feel threatened, remember God and what He has done for you time and again. Tap into the knowledge that nothing can withstand His power. Wait for His word. But if you find yourself already on the run, remember that He will provide for you no matter where you go. Just rest in Him—He'll give you hope and strength for the next steps.

Thank You, Lord, for providing for
me no matter where I go.

WATCH WHERE YOU'RE GOING

Let your eyes look right on [with fixed purpose],
and let your gaze be straight before you.
PROVERBS 4:25 AMPC

One way a woman gets stressed out is by not living in the moment. She's wondering about all the what-ifs. She's consumed by all the what'll-happens of tomorrow. And all the could'ves, would'ves, and should'ves of yesterday. But worrying about the future and ruminating about the past only serve to ruin her present. Not only that, but such distractions from the now set her up for a major fall because her eyes have left the path laid out for her.

The safer route is for her to leave all those stressors by the wayside. To focus on taking one step at a time, knowing that God intends for all things to work out for her good. No worries. Simply walk on the faith side—and let all else be.

Lord, give me the wisdom to watch my way, knowing
You have already gone before me and made
the path safe for my feet—and heart.

ABOVE THE STORMS

Peter got out of the boat and walked on the water and
came to Jesus. But when he saw the wind, he was afraid,
and beginning to sink he cried out, "Lord, save me." Jesus
immediately reached out his hand and took hold of him.
MATTHEW 14:29–31 ESV

At times, stress is like a storm raging within and without, drawing our attention away from God bit by bit. Then, when we suddenly realize our eyes are no longer on Him and our ears are deaf to His voice, we begin to sink. That's because we're looking at the waves instead of Jesus. We're listening to the howling wind instead of the Holy Whisperer. Before we know it, fear has supplanted our faith and we're in danger of drowning.

The remedy? Make Jesus your main attraction. Fix your eyes on the Water Walker. Keep your ears open to His Word. In so doing, you'll be riding above the storms within and without.

Jesus, help me keep You in the forefront of my heart
and mind, for You alone are my safe haven.

ATTUNED TO GOD

"Give in to God, come to terms with him and everything will turn out just fine. Let him tell you what to do; take his words to heart."

Job 22:21–22 MSG

How many times do we not let God in on our plans, run ahead of what He has planned, and miss the blessings He's waiting to pour out on us?

Perhaps it's time to stop trying to figure things out on our own, thinking we know best. Maybe our thoughts and feet should come to a screeching halt. This just might be the day we get it right.

Consider spending some time in the Word and in prayer, allowing God to lead the way. Know that with God on your side, everything is and will be fine. Open up your mind to the wisdom and insight He has for you. Store His words in your heart. Then, and only then, attuned to and in step with Him, walk on.

Lord, I'm so tired of trying to do all this on my own. Show me what You would have me do, be, and see.

SCRIPTURE INDEX

OLD TESTAMENT